Keshia
Thank
so much
supporting my

Peace &
Coffy Davis
2001

MEdusa

Reflections of an angry Black girl

By Coffy Davis

This book is Creative Non-Fiction. Names, Characters, Places and Incidents have been changed or modified to protect the innocent.

MEdusa

First Edition

Editor: Adrienne Oliver (Chapters 1-16)
Coffy Davis (Chapters 17-28 Outro & Prologue)
Cover Art: Quinton Thomas

T.U.R.N. PROJECT
Neighborhood Center of the Arts

Author bookings/Book orders CoffyDavis@yahoo.com
Website: https://jddavis7.wixsite.com/coffy

PRAISE FOR **ME**DUSA:

DEDICATION

This book is dedicated to my mom, Duchess and every unsung hero whoever had to deal with trauma while raising her children. I love you just as you are. This book is not to dishonor or discredit you in anyway but only to tell the truth and shine light on generations of pain and triumph, a journey that led us to the beautiful place we are in now.

HIT PLAY

MEdusa

ACKNOWLEDGMENTS

I would like to thank all the people who were instrumental in creating this vision; my mom Winni aka Duchess for her traveling grace, my dad, my aunts Lucille and Lillie, Sheila and Stan Futch, My son Khali and my husband Danny.

A special thank you to the people who inspired me and whose stories are intertwined with my own on this journey that we call life.

"Most people when they hear the name Medusa instantly visualize a scary snake monster with a face so terrifying that just one glance will turn a man to stone. Medusa's origins lie in North Africa where she represented one third of the Triple Moon Goddess. Ancient inscriptions about the North African Moon Goddess quote: *"I have come from Myself. I am all that has been and that will be, and no mortal has yet been able to lift the veil that covers me."*

- Silvestra Silvermoon

Intro:

N***** and Roaches

(A tragedy in 16 bars)

Intro.

Nobody stops. Nobody cares that we drag J-rock choking from the gutter, soaking blood into the sidewalk on the corner of Bancroft and High street.

Rewind.

This is Oakland. This is 1995. Nobody has more violence, more dope spots, more sawed-off shotguns more early morning police raids. We're doing what we do every night—chillin near the rag top Mustangs and Big Body Chevy's and posting up under the street light catchin this beat. We, ourselves, are art.

Nobody has more sparkling Dayton's; more customized paint jobs; more cannabis clouds wrapping around them.

Nobody has more *Cisco* and *Wild Irish Rose* blazing down their throats, numbing all sense of time and space. You lose time out here. You don't even know when the shooting starts.

And believe me, nobody looks better in *Guess* jeans and bra tops than my girl, Old-English-toned Deana standing with her hands on her hips laughing at J-rocks jokes." J" stands for Jerome and *Rock* cause he rocks shimmering chest candy and enormous diamond stud earrings, bright and shining like his teeth against his charcoal skin. His over-sized *Girbaud's* sag, weighted down with a pocketful of dirty dollars and $5 worth of weed.

We are Oakland's finest; paper bag brown kids. We're roses and thorns busting thru the asphalt in places so dark flowers ain't even supposed to grow. We are the Saturday night sidewalk revival in t-shirt's with mixtapes stuffed in the pockets of our Raider's jacket on one –ac-chord. We in tune with each other.

We are Gangster Nikes and *Coogie* sweaters crowding the sidewalks and gathering on the trunks of old school cars with reckless freedom waiting on the club to open. We are a church of bold colors and elaborate hairstyles singing praises out to fancy whips as they pass by metal shuttering, breaking sound barriers with their stereos. It's a jam session raging against the night on 14th and High Street where harmonies are built from the bottom up.

Verse.

This night started on a good note. I'm vibin with my homie Suinjata also known as Sin-for his wicked turntable skills. Sin leans on a blood red Caprice, coughing from indo smoke and burning his fingers on the roach clip before passing it to J-rock. We circle around the fellas showing off cut-offs and skintight miniskirts that cut so high up our thighs that brown butt cheeks peek-a-boo from beneath the spandex. We worship west coast emcees like gods and the music is our sanctuary. When it's really popping, when the bass from Mac Dre is pumping from someone's *Pioneer*, we inhale the bassline; we beat the rhythm down into our thighs like an 808-drum driving these boys wild with our flyness.

J-rock holds his heart looking at my booty, and delivers the lyrics to his same old song, "I'ma get dat ass. Feel me?"

"Fukouttahere," I scream back at him over the music in rapid AK 47 speech, double dutchin' my hips in tune with the quick tempo. I can't stand this dude. He talk too much. But my booty *is* rockin and I'm buzzed off cheap liquor and low budget compliments. My attitude is 40 proof like the *Cisco* that's surging like the BART train thru my veins. My temper is as flammable as the weed-*Baptized in eternal fire*[1]. My expression is concrete as a man's heart.

But the air is music. I got the rhythm of Fruitvale; the Jazz of Foothill Boulevard and I talk with a quick rhythmic bounce; beats and bars. Nobody got the mouthpiece like an east bay shorty and I got the ghetto-contralto honestly. We are a chorus of Ebonics and ghetto fabulous lyrics. Nobody has more culture, more ruckus, more ghost-riding, more side-shows, and more up-tempo bass heavy hip-hop in their swagger.

Remix.

It's all about timing. Tonight, the air is clear and laid back before violence shatters the darkness. There's no thunder before the bullets rain down. But you can feel the funk. Somethin's off key. I peep the crowd thinning out, the wave of tension building. I read between the lines of sudden silence; the split-second wind sucking out of the space that usually happens before the crack of gunfire; the 45 calibered fury. A quick succession. Tat. Tat. Tat. Tat. Then the surge.

Hook.

*Get that N****,*
*Yeah N****, Yeah!*
*Get that N****,*
*Yeah N****, Yeah!*

We get ghost. When the shooting starts, we run without direction. It's the breakbeat. We abandon *Louis Vitton* bags and *Motorola pagers*. We leave bottles of *Hennessy* smashing into the pavement and remix it with the sounds of screeching tires and gunfire. Nobody stops. Hundreds of kids scatter like roaches, half-drunk into late night traffic dodging bumpers and headlights. We're nothing but broad strokes and bold streaks. Horns playing high pitched screeches. Just footnotes. Scuffed

---

[1] Shakur, Tupac. Me against the world. Jive Records, Interscope Records. CD. 1995.

up K-Swiss diggin' into gravel around the corner. 5-inch stilettos squeezin' against the sides of buildings. A hub cap spinnin' to a stop in the street. Sin yanks me to the ground. My leg scrapes the sidewalk. I think fast. *Get up.* I jump up, bolt like lightening, run *boom-chick, boom-chick.* I bottle my screams up like brown liquor while I hide behind a light pole. But nobody knows nothing. Nobody seen shit.

And when I walk back down the street, scanning the ground, he's an island; alone. Fragmented into pieces cause the whole picture is too much for me; a Nike in the sewer, a trail of blood, red plastic cups, broken shards of images of teeth clenching, eyes bulging in terror and words drowning. He's litter clogging the storm drain. He's looking for sanity in chaos. We are broken into beats; kicks and snares; a fury of punches and kicks to the wooden door of the club. Sin starts yelling for a phone, "Open this fuckin door!" We hear people shuffling around behind the bolted door. Nobody answers. I grab J-rock by his *Karl Kani* shirt. He struggles to ask, "What happened?" Sin tucks an arm under his arm pit. We drag him onto the sidewalk. He's too heavy, we can't carry his weight. I fall to the ground with him. Sin runs back to the door, "Help us."

The Bridge.

Anger boils over, tipping him into full blown rant. Sin's unraveling. I never seen him like this. His is voice a broken rattle of riffs,

"Fuck...piece of shit ass. He gone die."

I pull J-rocks crumbled body into my lap. It's like pulling jagged scraps of him back together again. I sit silent feeling his shoulders shuddering, his fist clenched. He's talking non-sense...scats instead of words, "where I'm at? What happened?"

I don't know what else to say so I lie, "You fell"

He asks, "I'm gone play baseball?" *Baseball*? I remember the Spartan with the Big Stick in his hands swinging for the fence.

I try to rub the tension from his hands to stop his nails digging into his palms. His eyes roll into white. I rock his small head in my lap; slob wets my thighs where my skirt has ripped up the front. *My panties showing.* A bus passes by with blank faced passengers staring out the window at this urban dance of violence. Me holding J. Sin flailing his arms cursing like a mad dog and begging for help. Nobody does. Nobody wants to get involved. They see nobody but black kids with too much to drink, too much time on our hands and nothing better to do but kill ourselves.

This is Oakland. This is 1995. This is concrete and blood. This is us. This is the crossroads. This is where the weight of sorrow and pain come crashing in on you all at once. This is where bootleg emotions get dug up and you crumble like Sin into your palms and sob until there is nothing, but dry heaves left in your gut. We feel anger cut deep to our bones. We know nobody cares, because the way the police car rounds the corner with his lights off, because the door to the Endzone night club never opens, because I lay on the corner with J-rock gasping for air on my lap, cause his homies never come back to see if he's been hit. We never felt more alone. We never felt more shame. We sit waiting to hear ambulance sirens that always take too long. We sit wilting like flowers that just watched the sun refuse to shine down on us, and we know we will probably not survive the 90s.

J-rocks eyes have the familiar 1000-yard stare into nowhere.

I withdraw into numbness and let it envelop me.

Nobody lives forever.

Outro

1: **ME** Against the World

Now take my bitch
she won't complain about shit
cause she's my hoe
       -Too Short (Ain't nothing but a word)

      I have learned to accept the fact that I am a bitch. So, Too $hort's cock-strong lyrics beating violently in my Sony Walkman sings to me like an anthem; a ballad for broke bitches. The 72 bus is crowded. The driver hits the throttle. My all-white Keds skip on board and I toss $1.25 in change into the mouth of the metal box that counts coins and keep it moving.
      As usual, the bus crowd--buzzing like a jar full of nasty insects fighting for space--is thick. I fight my way in. I split the crowd like Moses. Lady bugs and irritating ass mosquito swarm around me. We're jam packed with kids on their way to school and worker bees on their way to the hive aka minimum wage job. A daddy long legs is dozing, mouth open and snoring loudly inside the collar of his Pendleton. I skip around his out-stretched loafers. A beetle-eyed Mexican is watching the pretty second-generation Latina grasshoppers with their *la Vida Loca* gear on full blast. I bee-line to the back past a squad of honorable Nation of Islam boys with steel fixed eyeballs looking fly in their bow ties. They stand confident like they have an arsenal of information in their brains. *Locked and loaded.* One righteous brother's gaze breaks ranks and peeps my femininity. I smirk. I get it all the time. I'm unsteady. I lean on the pole for balance and my mind flashes to a childhood song we used to sing on the playground... *the wheels on the bus go round and round.* I'm hovering on the metal bar and mean mug the dudes who sit in the rows of hard plastic AC Transit seats. Here they sit eyeballing my 18-year-old rump but can't conjure up enough chivalry to offer up their comfortable seat. I don't sweat it.

I'm used to it. Ain't no Prince Charmings around this way. I feel a tap on my leg and adjust my head set so I can hear the man tapping on my leg.

"How you doin?" comes from the ashy lips of a Hennessey tenor on a game hunt.

 This stank breath hawkish negro in Girbaud jeans with a transfer cuffed in his palm smiles from his seat. His smile is full of glass shard jagged teeth. I roll my eyes and turn my back to an angry, "Fuk you den biatch"

I pull the bell at my stop and don't look back, "Fuk ya mama, nigga."

Me and Oaktown got this strange love affair. I can't even front, the Bay is beautiful in early spring. It's the Oak Tree Town. They say it has the best weather on earth. The fog is rolling in from the bay. My body rocks in sync with the mellow yellow sky and the vibrant energy of the west coast. The coconut oil on my skin sparkles in the warm Mediterranean climate. I walk past street signs blossoming with a vineyard of graffiti. Oakland is covered in it. Helicopters strike across the sky like silver eagles. I pass a group of guys smiling my way. I hit them with a mean mug and keep walking. My wild mind fits in with the schizophrenic neighborhoods that polka dot from turf to turf and I know them by heart: 5-tray, the Twomps, Campbell Village, Sabrini park, Seminary, Dogtown... piss poor West Oakland with its ghost town and air perfumed with sewage. I look up and see the Oakland hills with its $300,000 castles in the sand. I pass homeless ensembles singing poverty hymnals in People's Park. The AC Transit bus drives off like a dragon breathing black soot into the air. The Bart train thunders beneath my feet like the underground railroad. It's Freedom. I rise and fall like the Bay's valleys and hills. Everyday I'm either all up or all the way down-- on the incline or decline.

The Town inhales your misery and exhales art and culture. On any given day the streets are alive with conscious sisters and brothers with dread-locks, House dancers in parachute pants, self-respecting Punjabi boys with their uncut hair tied into turbans, Fruit of Islam boys and Muslim Girls in Training, and Vietnamese kids. Oakland's slick as a fresh oil painting. I Look around from

7

the courthouse steps and it's like scoping a work of art with a dirty lens that captures the 170 foot Mormon temple, China Town with its fresh BBQ roast duck and pork hanging inside the window; and "the city jewel" the still waters of Lake Merit with its necklace of lights. In Oakland, ghetto kids pick fresh lemons from trees under blue skies and the purple sunset over the Bay is amazing. But it's a dysfunctional relationship. The Town is a scandalous two-timing goon whose sad truths remind you that it's an unrequited romance of blowing garbage, gap-mouthed empty storefronts, and a notoriously brutal police force. It's too late though. I'm in love with this run-down industrial shithole of a place. I'm lost in the insanity of love. I cross in front of a burnt orange Nova whose dreadlocked driver is banging Tupac,

> *I remember Marvin Gaye used to sing to me,*
> *had me feelin like black was the thing to be,*
> *And suddenly the ghetto didn't seem so tough...*[2]

The streets are crowded with Mustangs, z28's and Camaro's. I dodge relentless panhandlers and run up the steps of the courthouse that sits on the edge of Lake Merritt.

****

Alameda county courthouse feels like a tomb: dim and hot as hell. The courtroom is a boneyard of broken souls waiting with heavy hearts to be cast into the darkness of Santa Rita jail. I ain't trying to go to the Pen. It's a garden of hustlers, hop heads, crooks, and crack hoes. I'm on the docket today. I sit on the pews waiting on black Jesus in his velvety robe to call this chaos beating in my teenage chest to order. I try to relax but fear is a flame that burns slow in my gut. I try not to think about going to jail. A crackhead, with eyes dull as tinted windows, leans in, "You prolly ain't done nuthin but wrote some bad checks." She says with a dry

---

[2] Shakur, Tupac. *Strictly 4 My N.I.G.G.A.Z.* Jive Records, Interscope Records. CD. 1993.

chuckle. My mind runs wild with what ifs. Karma is a bitch that's running up on me quickly. I don't want to go to jail. I ask her what's going to happen like she's my attorney. And she gives good counsel, "If this your first time you gonna get probation. Ain't nothing to worry about." She sucks her dry rotted teeth. The inmates in orange jumpsuits are led in from the bull pen. I hope she's right.

Behind me I peep Eldron's dad with his jheri curl shag dried up tight to his scalp. Damn, last time I saw him he was parked at the elementary school getting some head from a tweaker. I wonder if he recognizes me. He's probably thinking the same thing I am, *Damn what you do?*

Hit a lick
verb
1-to gain a shit load of money in a short amount of time.
2- a robbery

"Robbery, forgery, embezzlement and fraud, how do you plead?" I shift in my shoes like I'm dodging a blow. There's a gust of memories of my petty crimes: slipping my hand into the white lady's Burberry handbag, hitting delete on the register and pocketing $35, engaging this dude with a smile big enough to make him forget his credit card on the counter, pillaging purses, pockets and people. He read my shit like it's a Grammy nomination for record of the year. "How do you plead?" *Ask me no more questions, I'll tell you no more lies.* He has a paternal tone to his voice, and it rumbles from his belly like thunder. It's the sound I remember my father making that one time he had to spank me. Pops had a belt in one hand and my ankles in the other while I hung upside down kicking and screaming like a wild chicken. It ended with both of us being too exhausted for the whooping. Thinking of my father is like detonating a bomb inside my chest. I know I'm prone to explosive tears. I'm tripping. I thought about this shit all night. I don't want to go to jail. *U.G.L.Y. you ain't got no alibi... you ugly*

I plead, "Not Guilty."

The best solo performance goes to me. I tell lies that should set my pants on fire. At 18 years old, I look like a school girl but I'm really a kleptomaniac who can disappear your credit card right before your eyes like a street magician. My sleight of hand is amazing. I'm an illusionist that can conjure a smile at the same time I sneak your card. I perfected my craft at the register at my job Grand Auto across from Oakland High School. Now you see your American Express, now you don't.

How can I explain to father judge that the 10 crispy hundred-dollar bills seemed life changing at the time? How can I approach the bench and argue to a man who makes more money in a day than I've ever owned in my whole life. The 30-40 dollars I hit the register for daily wasn't adding up to enough to stop the eviction process. So, I went for the big lick. I'd then have to explain that when Oakland PD came swinging handcuffs, I didn't know which petty crime the arrest warrant was for. That just a few moments before, my friend called with the news that plain clothes police were asking around for me in my old neighborhood. That I had just left Planned Parenthood with a slip of paper with 6-weeks pregnant on it and a handful of abortion pamphlets. How could I explain that I thought the cops might want to question me about my two friends that had been gunned down. I don't know if caged birds sing but I know they can't sleep. The night I spent in county was songless as shit. I stood thinking about the previous night of squatting over a metal toilet while a 17-year-old car jacker I befriended, watched my back. I struggled to shit in a crowded toilet area where inmates huddled together snorting coke had smuggled in in someone's coochie. I spent the night whimpering on a cot while forty or so women fought over the TV, farted, shit, and walked around with tits hanging like deflated balloons. I finally fell asleep to the sound of lesbian lovemaking. All I can say is, "I don't want to go to jail." I stand there with my arms crossed over my chest like armor. I stare at my feet. He looks down at me, "Young lady, uncross your arms! You have no idea about life yet. When you come in my courtroom you show some respect. Stand up straight. Look at me when I'm talking to you. That's what's wrong with the young people today they have no respect." I look him straight in the eyes, stone faced and cold. I don't care anymore.

He shakes his head, "I don't know where you get this attitude from." I see his face soften.

"I sentence you to college."

"Huh?"

He shook his head, "Where'd you get this attitude from?"

2: The Root of the White Oak tree in our front yard ran deep underground like the secrets women whispered by the kitchen sink in our house.

It was 1981. The Oak stood alone with its branches reaching out for God, experiencing life, death and resurrection all in one year's time. But roots also stretched beneath the surface of my family tree and gripped me to the floor. I was laying in the living room rummaging through my mom and aunt's conversation like most 5-year-old little girls do. They were sipping Brass Monkey, letting their backbone slide to Diana Ross, *Upside down, boy you turn me, inside out and round and round*[3]... I always loved when my mom sang Diana Ross spinning around wildly like a diva.

I was once told that roots can crack foundations, bust waterlines and lift concrete. I listened to the women burying family secrets in each other's dirt. I wondered if "Uncle" really had a "sex problem." Images of the things they described became troublesome weeds that ran wild in my imagination. I pictured uncle on top of my aunt doing "his business." They thought I was asleep, but I was gathering information like family jewels. This is how I found out who just got arrested, who didn't have any money and who was sleeping with whom. They covered the shame of infidelities in giggles. It seemed so exciting. I pocketed them like gems. Wore them like raggedy hand me downs. I heard my mom say it was just a phase that Uncle is going through. He's just in his prime. I didn't know what "prime" was, but it seemed special.

---

[3] Ross, Diana. *Upside Down.* Diana. Motown. 1980

To everything there is a season.

It was fall, the season when the soles of my feet crunched on thick leathery leaves that had floated from the trees. The time of year I would jump on my yellow Banana seat Huffy bike and kick around the metal pedals with my brother Mike yelling from the handlebars of my bike. The cool crisp days of winter when the humidity was gone. I could ride past neighbors hanging lights from their porch. We were dirt poor, but each day was bursting with potential.

The house was still. The women had trotted back to their rooms and slid into the arms of the ones they loved. That night I lay and closed my eyes and listened to the Cicadas singing their evening moonshine songs. Confederate flags blew in the cool Arkansas air. But Autumn in Arkansas is when the harvest comes. It's the end of the growing season; the occasion when men come from the fields to reap the crops.

According to the King James Bible, there is a time to plant and a time to uproot. My legs stretched out like stems sprouting from my Mickey Mouse night gown on my damp sheets. My gown was soaked and sticking to my flesh. I had wet the bed. My panties were crumbled under the couch out of sight. I was afraid my mother would be upset that I peed on myself again.

The floorboards groaned beneath his feet and he stopped at the foot of my pallet on the floor. His breathing was hot, heavy and humid as august. His skin was brown and staunch like smoldering hickory. He dug me out from my blankets, wiggled me loose and carried me quietly down the hall. His sultry smell reminded me of crouching with him outside near the bushes of our neighbor's houses. I'd trudged beside him quietly along the shadows of apartment windows while he courted glimpses of partially dressed women. It was a treasure hunt where my cousin Isiah scratched around the base of a house like a nasty rat looking for morsels to feed his sexual appetite. I was just a kid who'd follow my favorite cousin to the depths of hell if he'd let me. I didn't realize the depths of hell would begin here on my mother's bathroom floor. I was engulfed in the flames of fear as he laid me beneath the sink. My unripen vagina didn't even bare the early crops of hair. The linoleum was cold on my naked back. His eyes lit with excitement by my nakedness. He plowed his tongue inside me like a scythe lunging into the earth. When he broke ground, the taste of urine assaulted his tongue and he quickly retreated to the toilet gagging and spitting. He said with a hiss, "Don't do that again." I crawled back into my mind. My mom always told me I daydreamed too much.

In my mind, I climb over a fence and land in the woods with my brother. It's Fall. The leaves on the ground are beautiful reds and browns. I'm swinging on a vine above the creek where the mud puppies burrow into the mushy sand. I'm on my Huffy outrunning a summer storm.

I could no longer feel my hungry cousin licking the sap from between my legs. His tongue was strong, and his fingers raked against my privates. I stared at the space underneath the door wondering if my mother would wake up. He sat on the floor pulling and jerking himself while he stared at my legs outstretched like petals. He whimpered and I watched as milky white tears flowed from his penis. He smeared it against my thighs.

By morning I was back in my pallet with the urine and semen crusted over on my thighs. No one noticed. I buried the night in my mind. Thoughts lay beneath the surface and grip me to the floor. Memories cling to the structure of my mind and like ivy continue to grow over any surface.

The things my mother whispered about tear a hole in me. I wonder if she knows her cousin has a sex problem too. She planted kisses on my cousin. She loved him. I secretly loved him too. My mother's garden was a graveyard of bones.

3: Man-Hunt

Lawrence is a dusty ass fat boy who likes to cap on everyone he sees. He'll talk about your shoes, your clothes and everything else about you, your mama and your whole damn generation. He's like the class clown of the playground. Everyone is afraid of him, everyone except my skinny big brother Mike. Mike built his reputation as the junkyard dog for body slamming Lawrence on the playground for feeling on my bootie when we first moved here. He likes me. I see his fat eyes watching me play four-square in Emery Glenn. He sucks his bottom lip, "Your game sick." I know it is. I'm a beast in everything I do. Matt, a Vietnamese kid, is laying on the slide, "Y'all down for a game of Manhunt?"

I'm always down. I run with the boys playing *Man-hunt*; a ghetto version of *hide-n-go-seek* where there is no home base. It's a roguish game; a savage sport where only the strong survive. You beat the bushes, sweep the streets, do whatever you gotta do. If you're "it" you just run your ass off until you catch someone. We play over a stretch of blocks from the playground on 59th to the dope spot on the 6300 block. The thing is once you get caught, you're "it" too and now you have to help find the others. The game climaxes with a mob chasing one or two people. I run like Flo-Joe when Big Lawrence gets on my pink Reeboks. He's waiting to catch me slippin again but I'm quick. I'm fast on my feet. I got *Jungle juice* in my blood. I see Mike on his belly by the trash can. He shoo's me off. It's every man for themselves.

It's the black hot summer of '88, the year when the Bush Administration is putting too much money on the so-called "war on drugs." Meanwhile, us inner city kids are on the front lines of urban warzones in a fog of tech 9 toting kids, hostile cops, relentless crack heads and the constant sound of gunfire ringing in our ears. We struggle every day not to slip thru the cracks. *Step on a crack it'll breaking our mother's back*. It's the year my period came with a vengeance and my body falls in rhythm with the blood moon. The year my mother slaps me on the back and says, "You a

15

woman now."

I can feel the asphalt scrape my knees. I'm hiding out below the bumper of a chrome Monte Carlo with Tru's and Vogue tires. I'm behind our apartment complex we call, "The Condos." The Condos are really a 50-unit income-based housing development in the belly of a North Oakland hood where the grass seems greener. It's a sanctuary of swinging double-dutch ropes and touch football games. It's where boys spar in the streets. It's where I hit cartwheels in the grass near the old wooden sign with its real name, Emery Glenn, etched into it. It's where I once stood with a baseball bat as my brother Mike fought an army of neighborhood boys. It's where everyone found out Jen fights with the boys. *If you hit my brother, we all jump in.* I run pass my house, a two-story stucco town house where the sidewalk ends and ghetto bird's swing so low, they shake the ceiling.

We're AFDC Case #0007865 at the welfare office and I rip out paper food stamps to make change for push-pops from the ice cream truck. My Mom used to be in the Air-Force but spent more time on base and chasing men than with us. She met my father in Arkansas when she was in Jr. High and lied about giving birth to his first son, my oldest brother, Mike. Turns out Mike was by another man but by then she was already married to my dad. They eventually had me and my youngest brother, Chet. Now they have an off- again-on-again relationship. They approach parenthood the same way. Sometimes it's on but for the most part, it's off.

During *Man-hunt* most kids run with reckless abandon. I choose to hide out. I'm in the same spot where my mom fought a thief over her purse after her graveyard shift at Providence Hospital one night. Right before she started carrying a 22. in her waist. Now, I feel someone scrapping beside me. It's Deon, *Deon Marche*. My breath catches in my throat. I'm juiced. He's the freckled-faced boy who lives across the street from me that I watch from my bedroom window riding his skateboard over cracked sidewalks. I try to play it off, but truth is I'm sweet on him. When I see him, my heart skips like Whitney Houston's record. I wear out the grooves to *How Will I know* on my mom's *Pioneer* stereo

system. *There's a boy, I know, he's the one I dream of*[4]... His jheri curl is swinging to his collar. His freckles are glistening from his face like stars in a cloudless sky.
He swoops down close to my ear, "Hey tenda."
I give him a mean mug to cover my shyness, "Anyway."

But deep down I'm shook up. I'm frozen in time and so is he. It's like a current that passes from him to me whenever he's around. We like each other. Even my brothers know that. Deon's smile is beautifully honest. I lose my focus long enough to let Lawrence get the drop on me and now his big paw chops into Deon's back. Lawrence is standing like King Kong, "You it, blood." He looks at me like he broke up our little party. I'm pissed but I'm up out of there, raging against the night. I hit the streets with Lawrence running me down like a line-backer. It's cool. I'll get his big ass back later.

I'm standing outside in the playground with Mike and a few of his patnas from around Emery Glenn listening to them crack jokes. They just broke into the all-white private school by *The Condos* and stole textbooks and microscopes. They are too hyped over their loot. I ain't trippin on that. My mind is on Deon though. I daydream about him. The only thing I know about relationships I learned in kiddie songs like, *snips and snails and puppy dog tails*.
I got my white jean shorts rolled up and a paisley print shirt with my purse splitting between my A-cup breasts looking lavish in my gear. Deon peeps game. He got on his all black NWA fit. He licks his lip, "I want to be your man. Is it cool?"

I'm shy but I want him too bad to let my fear stop me. I shake my head and now it's official. I try to look girly. I want to be *sugar and spice and all that's nice, cause that's what little girls are made of.* Not like me. I'm more like sticks and stones that break bones.
I'm just standing here looking at Deon. I don't know what to do. I look at his moist lips and get goose pimples. I want to kiss

---

[4] Houston. Whitney. *How will I know*. Whitney. Arista. 1985

17

him, but I don't know how. *Me and Deon sitting in a tree, K.I.S.S.I.N.G...*

Damn. I imagined it a gazillion times. I even practiced on my stuffed animals. I just didn't account for the tingling that happens when he leans in and smacks a rough and sloppy kiss that consumes my lips. I'm stumbling over his tongue. My smile is wet with his spit. I don't even know how to hold his hand, but he grabs a hold of me and slides his fingers through mine. We walk around the park letting everyone know about our 62nd street romance. I feel strange. Is this love? His mom walks up and she's high as a kite, hips swaying to the cocaine blues. *My mother his mother lives across the street 1819 Blueberry Street*. He runs off. The street lights flash on like lightening. He has a curfew. I don't.

My brother and his friends have kicked off an impromptu game of touch football and I'm chilling on the wooden bench at the playground in front of my apartment. I don't even see the girl until she's blocking my view with her Neon pink *Just* jeans and a Jheri curl. Her hands are on her hips and she's standing on the black tarmac that covers the park. "What's yo name?" *Honeybabychild.* I draw back, "Why?"
Her eyes look like guns drawn so I know what time it is. I stand up and assume the position. I don't know her. Her face is all twisted and krispy like she's heated about something. She's a girl about my height, a little bigger in frame than me and attitude just as heavy. I'm not afraid. By now my brothers have stopped tossing the ball. They sense that I got some funk. They aren't afraid either. They know I'm a titan on the playground. But she hasn't backed down either.
She upper cuts me with one phrase, "Do you know Deon?"
At first, I'm taken off guard. I'm not familiar with the emotions swirling in my gut.

My throat tightens, "Yeah why?"

"Cause he *my* boyfriend." She sounds winded.

Now I'm dizzy. I cross my arms like it's a bullet proof vest. "Ok?"

Don't cry.

My stance even looks like defeat. But she isn't done swinging,

"My name is Krystal. I'm Deon girlfriend. He come over my house every day!"

She came to fight me, but I don't have any fight in me anymore.

She asks, "So what's up?"

My words disappear like vapors in my throat.

All I can throw out there is, "I go with Deon."

It's like tossing a foul ball. Now any other time I would've smashed into her cheek by now.
Lawrence is rolling, "I thought you knew." There's a line drawn in the sand now.
     I walk around her in a ghetto war dance and smirk. She doesn't know how close she just came to getting served.
          You can roll your eyes and stomp yo feet but this Black girl you shole can't beat.

She has the same facial expression like she isn't afraid to run up either. She smirks, "Aye, so what's up?"

I shrug. A smile breaks out on her face, "What's your name?"
"Jen."
"I'm Krystal."
"I know you told me that already. You Deon girlfriend," I say while rolling my neck.

     We built a truce on a game of four square and shut the whole playground down with our skills. I'm the server at first. I say, "Service, no chicken feet, spinning, baby drops or snake eyes," and hit the ball. It lands in the line of one of the other three squares. Krystal hit's it sharply into Mike's square and he misses it. She laughs, "You out homeboy." I like this chick. She's a short female with a stringy curl cut into a mushroom style and little Betty Boop lips. She walks on her toes like a Black ballerina. We are both bubble gum chewing, candy necklace wearing girls who like to dance.

I can't break up with Deon, though. After Lawrence shiesty ass tells him about my confrontation, he stops washing his curl and is at my window hella quick with activator dripping from his head begging me to stay with him. Turns out Krystal and his mom are junkies who cop drugs together. He met her by default and the two of them had forged a bond during their moms' crack-cocaine binges. Now there is three. Me and Krystal climb over the wooden fence in his yard and take turns exchanging nervous kisses with him. We go to the blue store and steal candy together like professional boosters. We cross our hearts and hope to die before we tell the painful secrets we share about our past.

KRYSTAL

I'm a show-stopper on the dance floor and Jen got moves too. We make MC hammer dances to our love group New Edition's new vinyl, "If it isn't love."[5] She has records. I got cassettes, though. We be at her house cold chilling cause her parents be gone all the time. I make Cabbage Patch and Robocop dances in Hammer pants and patent leather shoes. She's like, "That's tight!" Jen cuts into the carpet in her living room doing the running man in her mom's combat boots to our ghetto choreography. I like her cause she's rough around the edges, unladylike as my mother says. She's a small girl with a big attitude. She's loud and opinionated. She wears her hair fastened into a banana clip. I'm amazed that every inch of her bedroom wall is covered with torn out pages of Word-Up and Right-on magazines. She lets boys do graffiti all in her closet. She say her mom don't give a fuck. She digs MC Lyte like me. She like Kid N Play and Salt-n-Pepa too and we record hits from KMEL our favorite radio station. She think she Salt. I laugh at her blowing kisses at a two-page fold-out of Tiamok from The Last Dragon in his

---

[5] New Edition. *If it isn't love*. Heartbreak. MCA. 1988.

speedo.

I don't got too many friends so it feels good to meet her. We true home girls. We daydream about "Green-acid-wash-overalls," a dude we peeped at Emery Plaza who look just like Tiamok in a pair of acid wash green Guess Jeans. But my mind is really on her older brother, Mike. We nickname ourselves the Unique-corns. We usually practice at her house because I'm too embarrassed of mine. My mom is on dope. I live in a two-story apartment complex full of roaches and crack heads. It's the kind of place ghetto kids call ghetto. My mom is usually twisted and knocked out damn near in a coma while my two-year-old brother is tearing the house to shreds. I love my mom, but I hate her drug habit and what it does to her. When Jen finally comes up, she sits in the living room laughing at my mom's nasty jokes. She thinks my mom is cool from the jump. She trips me out when she says she wishes her mom was like mine? Whatthehell? We fight crack heads for my mother over dope fiend stuff. I didn't think she could fight at first because she wouldn't run up on me when I was gonna fire on her. I was buggin'. I thought she was trying to steal my man. But I see now. She doesn't even question why, she just jumps in swinging.

I feel like Jen lives the good life because she always has a smile on her face. Most days, I go to her house to escape when things at my crib get too wild. We practice our dance moves and save some change to cross the tracks and go to the shopping center. We resort to stealing when we realize we'll never afford it and seeing as how Jen is a serious crook. She steal like a crackhead. We even steal her mom's blue Hyundai and joy ride around the hood. We have something else in common too...we both go with Deon. Until she serves him a knuckle-sandwich one day for hitting her little brother Chet. Damn.

4: WAR Games play out like a nightly event in Oakland. I wake in a fog of red and blue police lights flashing outside my window. I rise up out of my day bed and peek out the shadeless window.

Mike and his two friends, Sean and Marcus are spread out making concrete angels on the pavement; their arms stretched behind their backs. Marcus' black Acura Legend has all its doors wide open and is surrounded by squad cars. A K-9 is sniffing out the back seat. A red- faced cop has a long shotgun's barrel pointed inches from my brother's nose yelling, "Turn the fuck around before I blow your gotdamn brains out." He's gonna kill Mike. No one's home but me and Chet. I open my window and scream out, "What's going on?" The police ignore me. I struggle to pull my jogging pants over my panties. OPD is jacking them up and dumping them handcuffed into separate police cars like sacks of potatoes. I walk up and a cop stands in my path, "Get back!" I'm trying to get around him. I'm yelling, "Aye what ya'll doin to my brother?" They ignore me. They won't let me speak to him. They roll off taking Mike to the police station, but we don't have an adult to get him out.

It's damn near sunset by the time I hear the door opening and Mike dragging back through it. He shrugs it off like it's just another day in the hood. He puts Self-Destruction single LP on the record player and zones out,

Down the road that we call eternity
Where knowledge is formed and you'll learn to be
Self-sufficient, independent...
So do not walk this path they laid
It's Self Destruction, we're headed for...[6]

---

[6] The Stop the violence movement. *Self-Destruction*. Jive. 1989.

My heart is relieved. Mike is my rock. My smile was never convincing enough for my father to stay around, but my brother was always there. He taught me to pop-lock and moonwalk on the linoleum floor in our kitchen. He taught me to make chef creations like coffee cake with milk, flour and sugar, cause that's all we ever had in the fridge. He took up for me when folks teased me because I still peed in the bed. While my mom was always in losing battles with one relationship after another, he's the one who taught me to win. He taught me to go ten rounds. I am five feet of built up frustrations. Me and him would have our little squirmishes when I was little. I always lost. But he taught me the first line of defense, "Nise," that's what my family calls me, "Don't let no dude hit you." When I fight kids in our neighborhood, I can hear him saying, "Wipe your eyes and stop crying." We are a team—me, him, and my younger brother Chettie who is 7 years younger than me and 9 years younger than Mike. Chet is dark, ashy and puny in stature compared to us.

Mike is slim and muscular like his biological father Wayne. But he has a bipolar incredible hulk heart. I am jean shorts, tennis shoes and 100lbs that cannot be moved. When some neighborhood boys steal Chettie's bag of Halloween candy, me and Mike track them down like bloodhounds. Mike looks me in my face like, "You cannot lose," If they hit one of us, "we all jumping in." He taught me to pick up a rock if I had to. If they get the best of you, "tomorrow you fighting again." Damn right.

When he was around, I wasn't afraid of anything, not kids, not heights and not even the dark. He fought off the real-life boogieman too. I remember sitting in the closet with him while two neighbors were looking for us for some sexual game. They found us hiding beneath dirty clothes in my mom's closet and asked us to come out and join them. I was shaking like a leaf as Mike reluctantly rose up in his Star Wars drawers, "I'll be back." I never forgot how shook he was when he returned with his small ribcage heaving heavily. He pulled me close and whispered in my ear, "Whatever they ask you to do, just say no." I shook my head with my frantic 6-year-old heart beating wildly in my chest. He grabbed hold of me by my boney shoulders shaking my plaits, "Listen to me. Nise. Say no okay." I shook my head ok. I was frightened but I could tell he was just an afraid little boy, too. He just had the heart of a lion.

5: Souls of Mischief sit on the bleachers sipping

Cisco and watching future ballers swing for the moon and hope to land among the stars.

We at the gate looking out into the field at Emery High like Oakland A's fans. But it ain't the way Joaquin smashes his bat against the metal fence every time he misses a pitch that has us caught up. He been doin that. He got anger issues like most of the boys at my predominantly Black school. We're leaning on the rusted old fence watching the guys on 53rd street. It's the hang-out for high school drop outs who get inducted into the dope dealing hall of fame and sport 5-tray on their shirts like a badge. The main spot is the house of the Steven's brothers who've each dropped out of school at some time or another. They post up at their crib across the street from the school and holler at the school girls on their way to class. I usually ignore them. I lean on the fence, the beads on my stringy plaits barely touching the collar of my shirt, my booty stuffed in some tight-fitting denim pants with zippers on the calf. A Puerto Rican dude named Juman is pumping N.W.A. from his radio,

She had the biggest ass that I ever seen
In fact, she was like Medusa, titties full grown
One look and your dick turns to stone...[7]

I'm in the 7th grade. I have typing with the youngest of the 5-tray brothers, Faygo whose girlfriend just tried to check me after class one day about her man. I'm a freshman and she had to let me know. What she doesn't know is that she almost ate dirt. I chill. I just got suspended for going to Rakim's jaw. But I ain't interested in Faygo or any of his brothers. They come to the games and attend almost every other school function except

---

[7] NWA. *One less Bitch.* Niggaz4Life. Ruthless. 1991.

class. I ain't into drop-outs. I'm into Scrilla, bread, mayo, money, cheddar. And there's a new hand on deck, a Jr. High guy who could've easily fit into New Edition or any other boy band. We hang on the fence and keep our eyes on the prize.

Maceo Smith. He has a short torso and strong jaws. His bow-legs and white denim jeans make him easy to spot across the field. He's stocky and walks with his head the same level as his back like a wolf. All us females follow Maceo around like he's Michael Jackson. First day at our school he caused pandemonium in my heart. He's mixed with Black, Indian and White. He has super long eyelashes, eyes that sparkle like diamonds and a goofy quality about his face. It ain't nothing foolish about him though. I heard he fights a lot. We got that in common. His cousin Jaime is locked up for shooting a dude in the head in front of the school. Maceo's like the best of both worlds, heaven and hell all wrapped up in one pretty boy thug. He carries a wooden handled hair brush in his back pocket to keep the waves in his high-low in line. I'm already sea-sick. Word is that he's been kicked out of every school in B-town or Berkeley as the squares call it. That's where he's from, and this is his last hoorah. He wears a 24k-gold herringbone, nugget rings and a Motorola pager like he has some dough. He posts up at the pay phone between classes and smiles at his fan club with this twinkle in his eye. I think he's a dope-boy. I can't even look at him for more than a second without bashfully turning away.

Me-My name is Jenny, super cool, you mess with me
ALL- you a fool
Me-I got this nigga, on my mind, you mess with him
ALL-yo butt is mine!

I wear my nickname, Jennie-*boe*, in bubble letters ironed on the back of my tee, peroxided gold highlights in my bangs and *Let's jam* hair gel sweating out my edges. I spit verses from *Kid n'*

Play and *Salt-n-Pepa* like it's nothing. I love music. I spend all the money I steal on Slick Rick and Keith Sweat cassettes from the Arab stores that sell bootlegs for $5. I kick it with music heads. We cut class to watch battle rap in the breezeway. This spot is also known as *The cut*, the grey area between buildings where teachers and staff barely venture. This is where the wild things are. This is where you go if you want to fight. The stone-grey walls have *NSO* scribbled on them in black aerosol cause we rep North Side Oakland. You bet not even step foot in my school if you aren't from the North. *The cut* is where the smokers meet to fire up a nickel bag of weed and players come to shoot dice games or run trains on hoochie mamas.

"Ya'll want to hit the dank?" Jesus aka Wop, everybody's Mexican homeboy holds out some bomb in a baggie. "Nah." I don't smoke. He rolls a joint on his Algebra book. I'm buzzing on Wild Irish Rose liquor that Delana opened up a pack of red Kool-Aid in. We call this concoction a Shake-um-up. I come to *the cut* when I'm cutting class. Unlike my friends, I'm in college prep courses with the smart kids. My teachers were sure I was remedial until I aced all the tests in the efficiency exam raising all the staffs' eyebrows in surprise. Now I'm taking upper level courses and they can't put me out. My brother Mike cuts class too but no one notices him slipping through the hole in the fence and heading to his homeboy Sean's house to play his new Sega Genesis. He drinks and fights too. Mike's just as bad as me and slicker than shit grease so no one suspects him.

I love the down beat. I love the sound of sneakers on the concrete. Today, *Fila* and *Diadora* sneakers surround my homeboy Shade with his high-top fade and Nike Cortez. He's slap boxing with words. He's a hood gladiator of the English language. He's a rapper all bars- no microphone. He hits the crowd with, "They call me S.H.A.D.E. from the ville/cause I'm shady for real/run yo bitch crazy with my skills." I got his black and white raiders jacket tied around my waist, driving his groupies insane with rumors of us

dating. I'm just his homegirl, though. I'm always the homegirl. I'm
here with my click, my die hard patna Krystal from the *Condos*,
Delana, Tia, Robin and Juraine. Delana is hood royalty with her
light-colored eyes, asymmetric body wrap swinging over her ear
and gold-plated door-knocker earrings. Delana's hella fresh
standing knock-kneed with her hands in the back pocket of her
knock-off *Guess* Jeans with the upside-down triangle her and her
sister have sewed on. Her shirt has *Poison* spray painted on it. She
keeps her hands on her hip so the boys can glimpse her big ole
booty. *Never trust a big butt and a smile*[8]. She's the one
introduced me to *415 Click*[9] and gave me the cassette tape like it
was a bible. Now I worship Richie Rich like ghetto gospel. She's
always up on the latest fads too. She has her eye on a ball player
named Huey who shows her no love. My Puerto Rican patna,
Robin's here with her complexion the color of *Boricua* dust. She's
slender and tall with loose curls like the palm trees by the Bay
Bridge. Tia is the one with big titties. Her body is banging and
drives the boys crazy. She always got some boy trying to feel on
her. She got that Coca-Cola shape from her mama who's a drug
addict and prostitute. I found out the night we were coming from
a boat cruise and the boys pointed her mom out on the hoe stroll
while Tia just sat there like she had just saw a ghost. Her mom's
hustle keeps her laced in the tightest gear though, so I rock her
outfits to school too. And then there's Juraine, my Jamaican friend
who still has her heavy accent from the Bronx. She makes this
poor Jamaican cuisine of sardines in hot sauce and shares it with
us for lunch. We are the goof troop. We kick back and giggle
while the other girls stand around looking grown and smoking
joints. Someone hits play on the radio and *We Want Eazy* is
coming out the speakers. I know the words and I rock them...

---

[8] Bell Biv Devoe. *Poison*. Poison. MCA. 1990.
[9] 415. 41Fivin. Big League Records, Inc. 1988.

a brother who's smooth like a criminal
I mean subliminal
Otherwise known as a villain[10]

Maceo's here with his pack of wolves. That's the reason I'm here. He's like a sun that we orbit around. When the dice stops rolling, he snatches his money off the ground and nods to Que. Que is his cousin from East Side O. He's a boy in my grade with teeth like a canine. He introduces him to Robin because he thinks they make a good match. I die when Que writes Maceo's number on her Steno pad. I smile but my heart plunges into Death Valley. I glimpse myself in the glass by the door. My hair is just recovering from my mother's chop off and now the low fade is barely enough to put into a banana clip. Her hair's blowing like ribbons at a fair. I'm invisible beside her wild beauty and lush curls. I'm boney and fidgety; an ugly duckling with no grace. She's slender yet curvy. I'm chicken bone skinny like a young boy.

I'm the one that told her about him in the first place. I was walking to my locker when I first got snagged in his smile. My heart has been beating for him since he first came to this school, but Que doesn't think I'm attractive enough. Maceo just stands there, his smile sunshine in the fog. Robin is happy holding his number like she won the lotto. Meanwhile, I'm just a fly on the wall.

We don't even wait on the curb for the 72 bus we just kick rocks. We're always a dollar short for AC Transit. We wave to Robin who lives on 5-tray next door to the drop-outs. She's the only one with a backpack. She's forced to wave to us from the porch where she stands with her over-protective mother. Her mom hates us and doesn't like Robin hanging out with anyone who is not a Jehovah's Witness like them. It's 3:30 and we walk eight blocks down San Pablo Ave after grabbing fries for 99 cents from Giant Burgers. Juraine douses the big bag full of ketchup and

---

[10] Eazy-E. We want Eazy. Eazy-Duz-it. Ruthless. 1989.

we keep it moving. Tia jaywalks across Stanford, titties bouncing, to her house. We skip across the busy intersection at Stanford by the Nation of Islam boys and switch even harder singing in harmony, "Lil Sally Walker walkin down the street, she didn't know what to do so she jumped in front of me." *Gone girl do your thang.* I shake my butt for the Muslim boys. By the time I make it home the rotary phone rings.

Robin's afraid to dial Maceo's number. She's in a panic. I offer up my services. I got the gift of gab. "I'll call." She hooks us up on the three-way. I'm shy in person but on the phone I'm a beast. I can hear Robin breathing heavy while the phone rings. When I hear his voice my heart skips, but I rise to the occasion, "Maceo?"
" What's up, who dis?" I like his voice. It's like a heavy bassline.
"Jen."
"Who?" *the one that's been crushing on you forever.*
I talk fast because I know he's irritated, "Jen. Robin's friend. She wanted me to call…"
"Jen? Which one are you? The one with the dot on her forehead?" Juraine has a mole on her forehead.
"Naw that's Juraine. I'm the one with the gold bangs."
There's an awkward silence. "Aw shit. Salt n Pepa! The one with the pretty smile?" My heart skips like an Al B. Sure record.
I can tell you how I feel about you nite and day[11]
I'm stuck. *What the hell.* I can't even talk. He goes on, "The short one that's bow-legged?"
"Yeah."
"You the one I like. What's up tenda?"
The call comes to a screeching halt when Robin smashes her telephone in its cradle in breakneck speed. But not before I heard the magic words. My heart does somersaults. Juraine is leaning over my shoulder, "What he say?"

I steal Maceo like the candy bars we lift from *Bottom's up*

---

[11] Al. B. Sure. *Nite and Day*. In Effect Mode. Uptown.1988.

Liquor store across the street from the school. *What's up? How does it feel? I can't describe this feelin'*[12]

The next day he's walking me home. He's cool as the Bay breeze. I like that I can be myself around him. I'm young and wild. He likes my skin color. He says it's a pretty reddish brown. I feel tall as a California Redwood. My rowdy tom-boyish ways and flip mouth don't turn him off either. He likes my ghetto poor chick style and how I cut holes in old jeans and wear fishnets underneath. I find out he lives with his grandmother and she's blind and half senile and doesn't know what he's up to half the time. Cool. I invite him in. My mom's never home anyway. According to Slick Rick, we got this teenage love thing going on from day one. We fill up trash cans of water balloons and go crazy on my Vietnamese neighbors. Northern Cali is in a massive 3-year drought and we don't care. They join in the battle royale. I like that Maceo's really a goofy kid like me. Oh, but he does sell dope.

****

He's at my house tying off heroine in balloons to sell while I'm running around crazy excited about this stash of water balloons I have. I just kicked his ass in a pillow fight after he mowed Juraine down. I never seen a dude so young handle dope like a pro. After he finishes cutting and packaging his Hop, he runs outside to meet a firestorm of balloons from me and Juraine. He's under heavy fire. He hits the side of the house running like 5-0 is on his scent. We're on him. Juraine drops the trash can and chases him down until he collapses in the grass. He's squealing, "No Maaaan!" I run back to the sink to refill our supply for round two. I'm so amped. I have about six balloons already ready. When I hear the door open, I think it's Juraine. I turn around in my kitchen to find Maceo standing in the doorway with a big ass smile on his face. "What's up blood?" I'm chilling because we're in the kitchen. Worst case scenario, he's gonna rob me of my stash. I

---

[12] New Edition. *If it isn't love*. Heartbreak. MCA. 1988.

underestimate his thuggery. He runs up and tosses a whole trash can full of water over my head. I'm bopping around like a fish out of water, slipping and sliding on the floor. His roguishness is amazing, "My mom is gonna beat my ass!" I'm rolling. My mom's kitchen is flooded and Maceo and Juraine are in amp mode. She's chasing him down and hitting him all upside his head with balloons. Balloons fly into the walls and couches in the living room. I got tears in my eyes. I'm laying on the floor laughing so hard my stomach hurts. "I'm in hella trouble."

****

I stay in trouble. Me and Maceo take our antics to school. I find out he's a savage like me. No one knows the culprits, but we are the water brigade. Now I'm sitting next to our principle Mr. Shephard or Shepdog as we so eloquently call him. He's a six-foot-tall white guy who has no chill button. Shep wears binoculars around his neck and carries a bullhorn. He'll run us down at the liquor store or the donut shop across from the school. He's a one-man swat team that will get the drop on your ass quick, fast and in a hurry. You can't even run off because his binoculars can scope you 100 yards and running. Now Shep's telling me I have detention, as usual. He's so busy looking for my name on his hit list that he doesn't see Maceo's arm sling from around the corner and unleash a balloon bomb that explodes on impact in his lap. But I do. While Shep is running around like a mad man declaring war on who ever had the audacity to do such a thing, I'm rallying up the troops. Juraine and Robin, who is now over the Maceo dilemma, are on deck. We load up an arsenal. But the bell rings and renders my whole squad inoperative. They grab their bags and head to class. Robin's mom has her so shook she can't be late to class. But I'm not dying. Maceo should know me better than that. He doesn't. He lets his guard down too and heads to 5th period, Mr. Buckley's science class. My lunacy is undetected in the mass of students streaming into the open doors. I pass Mrs. McKinney's Algebra class and her suspicious gaze. I pass Mr.

Abrami our Italian coach who teaches Health and we swear is a mobster. He smiles at me. I give him a sweet smile back. By the time I'm at the door, Mr. Buckley, a pot-belly white guy in glasses, is standing at the chalk board preparing his lecture. I see Maceo sitting at his desk like a mark trying to look all studious with his arms folded on the wooden top. I holler, "Aye fool." Before he can say, "Hell naw" a balloon is already in pursuit. I rain two more balloons and turn on my heels and hit the bricks. I'm drunk on adrenaline. I don't even care that Mr. Buckley is on his wall phone before I'm down the hall. Maceo is soaking wet. His books are covered too. He knows he fucked with the wrong one. Shep is raging over the loudspeaker, "Jennifer report to my office nooooowwwwww."

I won't have sex with him though. He wanna sex me up but I won't let him. No matter how many times he holds his sac and squirms that I'm giving him blue balls. No matter how many times he say's "I'm tryna fuck." Even though his mannish fiery scent perfumes my bed when he lays on it listening to Boogie Down Productions. KRS 1 warns me in his song, *Ya know that's why, (loves gonna get you)*[13] His neck kisses burn holes into my composure. I'm scared. I'm not afraid of him. I'm afraid of sex. I want to be with him but when he comes after me for sex, I'm paralyzed by fear. I keep him off me, while my friends tumble around with his friends.

My big brother Mike comes home from his new job working at the Country club. He sees Maceo stretched on the sofa fooling with the answering machine. He doesn't realize we're trying to erase Mr. Shephard's message that he left informing my mother that I am suspended, yet again. Maceo talks trash about Mike every time he sees him in his slim fitting khaki pants and black and blue JC Penny's jacket. Today is no different. I'm gassed up describing slapping Marlon in 1st period. I was scared shitless, but my fury got the best of me. Marlon secretly likes me but got

---

[13] Boogie Down Productions. *Love's gonna getcha*. Edutainment. Jive. 1989.

mad because I won't let him finger bang me after school. I was tired of him telling people he was gonna slap me, so I jumped across the desk and got the drop on him. *Stick and Move.* Now I was a legend. Marlon was the crazy dude that almost beat a dude's brains out with a two-by-four in the gym. No telling what he would've done to me. But my brains beat brawn. I had already seen Shep in the hall, so I knew whatever beat down he had for me wasn't going to last too long. Turns out I was right. I fired on him in front of the whole class. Maceo loves my gangsterism. He calls me George Foreman. We sip from my mother's box wine and laugh. He smirks, "Don't even trip. I'ma erase this shit."

Mike pulls me into the kitchen, "Nise, why you got this fool over here?" He's whispering so Maceo doesn't hear him. He's heard about his family and his dipping and dabbling in drugs. Maceo also claims a set and has run in's with different crews. Nobody in Oakland really gang-bangs, they are just dope sets and streets are run by certain crews. Maceo claims Waterfront a Berkeley set. So, when boys on the corner see him, they start set tripping. My brother doesn't like me fooling around with this type of dude. I don't get involved with all that. I just shrug and say, "He's cool." I like Maceo because he's fun. I see something young spirited and outlandish lurking in him. I love how he talks. He has this deep, yet mellow tempo where words just drag out like it's coming from under a needle on a record. Most of the stuff he talks is just him high sidin. He comes skating with me even though he just rolls around slow with his arms out-stretched like he's trying to keep balance. He got wild eyes that blaze with excitement. I like the vibration of his laughter, it's deep and resonates with my spirit. I like him because he kicks it with me at school even though he's a couple years older than me and his homeboys think I'm goofy. He likes me, I think, because I'm goofy. I'm childish and fun and just like him, I don't give a fuck. I am Jane of the Jungle. Shera in the lunch room scuffle. And he is He-man.

Robin gets shot on San Pablo Ave. She's crossing the street

from 5-tray to her grandmother's house on the other side near Anna Yates elementary school. I catch wind of it by kids running in the halls shrieking and crying when I make it to school. Her cousins Terry and Valerie are crying by their lockers. I'm in shock. *What the hell?* Maceo tells me what went down. One of the 5-tray brothers, Enrique, found her slumped by a tree near the spot. No one knows who did it or why. After being shot, she had wobbled back across the intersection attempting to make it home. She thought someone had hit her in the chest with rocks. She told Enrique it felt like pebbles were thrown at her. Enrique picked her up and carried her home to her mom. There are no school counselors to explain shit to us. We just walk around like zombies. Frustration is setting in. My C-average drops lower. I get kicked out of College prep courses due to attendance. I get into another fight. This skinny long-legged dude named Gerald touches my butt and I follow him into the boy's bathroom, chase him into the stall and hit him with both barrels. I'm enraged that he touched my body. He had run his finger from my butt hole to my coochie while I was bent over going in my backpack. I lose it. I exercise demons of my past with my fist.

Maceo cusses out Mr. Wilcox in the computer lab. I try to set the trash can on fire but fail. Juraine stops talking to me after she runs away from home. She lives with Delana now cause Delana's mom takes everyone in off the street. It's awkward. Everything is in a tailspin. And then Maceo gets put out. There's no warning. He's cleaning his locker out before I even make it down the hall. His face is tight. His eyes are blank like the flames have been choked out. I was going to say something, but I am dumfounded when I see tears in his eyes. The air is thick as ganja smoke. I think we can fix whatever happened, "What you do?" He won't talk though. His words are probably jumbled in his throat like mine. He's just tossing books into the hall while security sucks his teeth nearby. I try to put out the flames, "It's all good. You probably just getting suspended like me." He punches the locker, 'It's over for me now." It's like he punches me in the gut. He has called the gym teacher, Ms. Sakraida, "A stupid ass bitch," and now it's over. This was his last chance. No other school districts will have him. I can see pain flexing in the red veins on his face. He spits out, "I hate this fuckin school." I suspect it's not hate that swirling in his belly. Remorse is the fatigue that sets under his eyes. He's crying in full throttle now, face red and snotty. My wounds are bleeding out too. I start crying because I have built my days around him since I met him. We're friends, nothing more but most certainly nothing less. I only French-kissed him once in the yard of the private school when we were spray painting on the walls. Mike was with us, so it was a brief sloppy kiss that ended with Mike threatening to fight him for kissing his sister. As of now, he's the best friend I have. The one who I carry in my heart to bed when I use my fingers to rub out the pulse between my thighs. The one I dig up in memories while I look at my wall decorated with posters. He's the one I defend when adults talk about how bad he is, or boys talk about wanting to fight him. He's the one I sneak in and let curl up on the purple crush velvet couch downstairs at the *condos* cause he don't want to go home to a virtually empty house.

Now he is the one that security is escorting out like a hoodlum. He thunders by. There's this eerie rustling sound coming from his core. His voice trembles when he says bye. I know his life is changing. So is mine.

When he leaves the evergreen trees in front of the school blaze like torches and burn to crispy black spears.

6: Potholes In My Lawn.

7.1 is the magnitude when things fall apart. Things like books and dishes topple from shelves.

Sometimes you hear a buzz before a quake that causes terror to suspend you in time. It's similar to when the stressed and unstressed notes of a scream tangle like tumble weeds overrunning your throat; when emotions splinter but won't shatter and the words lay hanging against the frame in sharp fragments. This is what shakes the foundation loose and sends things hurling into each other. Then there's silence. Disaster strikes suddenly. You don't even hear birds singing.

Maceo disappears into the game for a while. I don't even know where he is when the earthquake hits. With an Earthquake there's a sudden release of energy from the earth's crust much like the wave rushing through the stadium at Candle Stick Park during the 1989 World Series. Kind of like the rush I got when I first met him. I hear that the shake of an earthquake can destroy many structures you once thought were solid; unbreakable. The force of the 1989 Loma Prieta Quake hits San Francisco Bay Oct 17 at 5:04 pm and causes the Bay Bridge to crack at its seams and the double decker Nimitz freeway by the Cypress Street viaduct to pancake into itself. Cracks splinter into buildings. Glass shatters into the streets. Nothing is the same anymore.

Relationships are like that. My parent's rekindled romance is short fused. It starts with petty arguments and small scuffles in the hallway. My father works a lot but is always broke. He hates to be home. My mom meets his disinterest with childish antics. She picks fights and hides his things. He's yelling, "Duchess where my damn keys?" while she claws at him and tries desperately to get any reaction, she can will from him. Her voice is whiney and soggy as a diaper. I hear them tussling around in the hallway every night. She knows where the fault lines are. She tries to insult him.

Her words are like tiny torpedoes to a man who is emotionally cold. I find his keys for him. No need to try to make a man stay around that don't want to be here. She cries for him to stay but he blows out with the fury of a natural disaster. I know he's going to leave again. My family is at the breaking point. Fear of him leaving is a shadow that follows me around. I blame her.

This day it's hot as a crack house. That hot humid Indian summer heat with a quiet yellow sky. I'm in my bedroom undressing, pants around my ankles when I hear the whistling. It's like the world stops turning for a fraction of a second. It's silent as death. There's a bizarre feeling before a quake. It's like the quiet before the storm. I know that something is about to happen. I sense it. I stand tense with my pants dangling at my ankle and strain to listen to the earth's distress. The humming is growing louder and angrier.

Suddenly, I'm lifted from the floor in a sudden burst of rage and tossed back down to a rolling sea of carpet. I struggle to get my balance and pull my pants up. I turn in circles and try to grab ahold of something, anything. Everything is moving, shaking, rolling. I hear crashing and glass shattering. I see my bedroom door swinging open in its frame, so I dart through it and bolt to the stairs. Before my foot can leave the landing, I freeze and fall back. The stairs are an ocean that's ebbing and flowing with steps. I hear Chet yelling from his room. I dash his way. I find him on the floor sitting in a pile of Nintendo wires with his little arms trying to hoist the TV back onto its stand. I yank him by one arm out of the way of the falling TV and leap like a frog to his bed where we huddle until the shaking subsides. It seems like forever but in actuality it's only 60 seconds.

Then it stops. Just as quickly as it started. My legs are Jell-O as I drag my brother down the stairs and pour into the mass of people who mirror my frantic eyes. My mind is jittery. Thoughts are fractured images of worry. *Where's my parents? Where's Mike?* It's madness. There's people running around searching for others. Some are in a stupor. Transformers explode in burst of green.

Electrical wires have broken from light poles and some are flickering in the street like sparklers on the 4th of July. Chettie's shivering beside me. The ground shudders underneath our feet. Our Vietnamese friends have a weather radio that they crank up. Everyone's tripping out. I catch scraps of what's going on, *The Bay Bridge fell. The Freeway collapsed in West Oakland and has people trapped inside it.* I see Mike and Big Lawrence walking huddled close together. It's getting dark and no one has lights. Our neighbors feed us. My parents finally make it home. It's a restless night. I sleep in the door way dressed in a sweat suit and tennis shoes. My mother tells us we have to be prepared to bust a move. She tells us that we can't get too comfortable. We never know when we'll have to leave. I don't sleep.

The aftershocks are terrible. One sends my head smashing against the wall. For the rest of the night I lay awake listening to Lancia's Invisible *man* on the radio. In the play a scientist is able to make himself invisible. I think it must be a wonderful thing to be able to hide in plain sight. When chaos erupts around you, to be able disappear in the shouting and crying and collapsing of things. Still, sometimes the aftermath seems greater than the actual disaster. They say the epicenter is where the largest vibrations are felt. I feel it banging in my chest when my father packs up and heads back to the South. Funny thing is, even when he is here it feels like he's miles away. My heart aches for him. The days following his departure, I'm in a blizzard of emotion. The water recedes and I'm deserted on the shore. Now, the only thing I have left of my dad is a box full of his clothes and the lingering scent of his Lagerfeld cologne.

What to do when you die?[i]

De La Soul. Potholes in my lawn. 3 Feet High and Rising. Tommy Boy Records . 1989

7: Gold Digger

Maceo no longer pretends to be a student. He's a full fledge drug dealer. He swings by the school in his new Mustard colored Mustang with shiny rims and I dip out with him whenever I can and watch him touch the wires together under the steering wheel to fire up the engine. There's no pretense that we are anything but friends now. During the summer I spent a few weeks in Detroit, Michigan with family and although I blew his phone up with calls every day, he managed to sleep with two of my friends. The same day. I was crushed but we both know the real. I ain't trying to give up the punany and he ain't trying to wait. So, I mob with him from time to time, but it is what it is. I'm still his homey, as he puts it. I'm down to earth. I'm cool. All the boy's think I'm cool like that. The perfect homegirl. He buys me lunch. He blazes dank when we ride, and we steal batteries and tags from parked cars. We are Bonnie and Clyde or maybe Dick and Jane, cause yeah, he still wants to fuck.

Me and Delana are thick as thieves, literally. Krystal's staying home more and more from having to deal with her mom's drug use. When her mom goes to jail, Krystal doesn't come back to school. I beat Juraine down in my doorway before she moves back to New York and Delana, who had set it all up, watches. I was tired of the argument scrimmages and just went to war. It's scandalous like that out here. One minute we're friends the next minute I'm smashing your head into floor. But me and Delana remain cool.

Me and Delana are walking across the tracks in Emeryville to a new theater they built in Emeryville Plaza. She wants to find a job. Her parents barely have enough money to feed her and her 13 siblings. Not to mention her mom, Ms. Patty is like Mother Theresa of the hood and picks up stray kids whenever duty calls. I have no idea why I'm tagging along. I never really thought about getting a job. I babysat around the *condos* for change here and there. I stole whatever else I needed. But now Delana has me coming with her on a job hunt. I want to go to *Tower Records* and steal some tapes. I'm in rolled up jean shorts and a tight-fitting top with a plunging neckline to show off my budding breast now that I'm no longer on the itty-bitty-titty committee. No need to stuff tissue in my bra anymore.

In the lobby of United Artist Movie Theater, I twiddle my thumbs when a tall Black guy escorts her to the back. Delana tried to dress all professional and shit with a wrinkled K-mart blouse tucked into a long khaki skirt. I catch him looking my way with a strange look on his face. I lean back in the chair, kick my *Keds*, and wait while Delana's interview lasts a good ten minutes. Soon, Delana's smiling walking back up with the guy on her heels. When I stand up his eyes light up a bit, "What's your name?"

Pudding tang and if u asked me again and I'll tell u the same

I shoot a glance at Delana, "Jen."

He looks me over again from head to toe before smirking, "You want a job?"

Hell yeah. "Yeah that's cool." I look back at Delana like *what tha?* ...

He tells me he's the manager, Mario. He motions for me to follow him into the back. I do. I sit down in a metal chair while he closes the door behind us. He doesn't sit at the desk, but he pulls a chair right in front of me and stares into my eyes. I want to look away, but I don't want him to think that I'm not confident enough for the job.
He licks his desert dry lips, "How old are you?"
"Sixteen"
He's looking between my legs at the way my shorts ride up into my cooch. I close my legs and sit like a lady.

He continues with the interview, "Tell me something about yourself."

I struggle, "I um… I'm in school. I go to Emery…"

He cuts me off, "What do you like to do for fun?"

Huh? I think to myself; *I like to smoke beedies and fall out giggling drunk on Shake-um-ups with Delana. I like Red vines and Salami sandwiches from the Blue store. Dafuq kind of question is this?*

He cuts to the chase, "You gotta boyfriend?"

"No."

I walk out with the job. Mario and his assistant manager Kirk stand together watching me and Delana leave.

I love my first real job. I'm good at the concession stand. I learn the register super-fast. All the girls who work here are young like me and very attractive. I work 8 hours a day seven days a week for $4.25 an hour. I'm dizzy tired. I call orders in my sleep. One day Tupac Shakur comes in. He's a local rapper with the Bay Area group, *Digital Underground*. He has a Gumby hairstyle and one of the legs of his jeans is jacked up on one of his skinny legs. He has a big charismatic smile. I'm hustling hard to fill my orders, but his entourage goes to another server. All I can do is watch him in awe. He has a light in his eye. He's animated like fire, warming the room with his energy. I heard he is filming a movie called *Juice*. I know it'll be good. I watch him walk down the hall to the theater with confidence and swagger and wonder what it's like to know you will be on the big screen soon. He looks so normal. I want a guy like that, someone who enflames me.

It's hard for me to skip out and catch movies like the other teens who work here because Mario is always on my ass like a bread crumb trail. I work right under him. I met a friend guy named Jaime who walks me home and tags his name in my closet and creates graffiti on my door that Picasso couldn't fuck with. But Mario watches him, too. He starts scheduling us at different times. But I'm always on Mario's watch. He's standing behind me while I load the popcorn bins. He's in my ass while I'm refilling the drinks. He's breathing on my neck when I'm stuffing nacho trays. I catch him eye-balling my figure all through the day like a vulture flying over a carcass. It's getting hard for me to rob the register and the *Will Roger's* donation jars. I try not to make eye contact. Every time I smile, I fear it's seductively. Everyone's starting to notice and starting rumors about me and him. I'm not fooling around with him. Mario's not bad looking though. He's a twenty something year old guy whose nut brown with broad shoulders and a boxy head like a Rottweiler. I don't really know if I'm attracted to him. He's always in my Kool-Aid, though.

Tonight, is the opening night for the movie *House Party* and we're all juiced. I'm cute with my work shirt tied in a knot on my back showing my belly. Mario announces that I can go sit in and watch it but before my ass is comfortable in the seat cushions, he's right beside me. His hand is in my lap and he's strumming my pants leg like a guitar. My heart is palpitating with the same rhythm. His egg breath is hot in my face. Delana is sitting with Kirk and she's gung-ho about his attention. Kirk has a curly fade like he's in the R&B group *Troop*. Both him and Mario are dancers and they come to our school dances to perform in Lug boots and Fubu. I don't know if Mike thinks I'm pretty, but he definitely wants to get down with me. I can sense it. I let him feel on me. *This old Man He play one, he plays knick knack with his thumb, with a knick knack paddy wack give a dog a bone...* I flinch. His fingers are pulling a trigger. He's setting off memories that flash at point blank range. I can't enjoy it. By the time the movie is over he's begging me to leave with him and Kirk. Delana's eyes are pleading. She's whispering to me, "Come on Jen, you know I been wanting Kirk." Mike is standing by hoping that Delana can coach me into coming. She's supa dupa fly with her *Kanekolon* weaved hair style and she isn't tryin to let it go to waste. I don't think he realizes that I'm a virgin...kind of. I don't go. That night we make it to her house late, clothes wrinkled to be damned, and her mom meets us on the porch with open hand slaps, "Y'all nasty ass cows! You been out fuckin?"

I'm stunned. I'm a virgin. Delana's a hot girl, though. We call her "Big Fats" cause she got a big fat ass and she keeps getting thicker. She got some big juicy hot lips outlined in black liner and she's always smacking when she talks. She's more daring than me. Her and her younger sister Queen (short for LaQueen) and Krystal go to the *Sideshow* on Bancroft looking for high rollers. It's a Saturday night hang out in the Eastbay where guys show off their tricked-out cars, sidin', hitting switches on hydraulics and doing donuts and other stunts in empty lots. It's a fashion show of candy paint and shiny rims. Maceo tells me the Sideshow is a candy store for Gold diggers who like guys with money. He's a regular. According to him, young hoochie mama's, old hoes, loud mouthed skeezers and trifling hood rats all parade their best outfits up and down the strip on Bancroft. Even though Queen is only 14, she's money hungry and more eager than Delana. Queen's a pretty golden yellow girl with dimples and a dangerously sexy swing in her hips. Most of the time they are just window shopping. But Krystal met her boyfriend Dlynn there one night and on my way to school I marvel at his royal blue Cutlass parked outside her house. He's 19, sells rocks and lives there now with her and her mother. I envy her. She doesn't even have to come to school anymore. Delana and her crew stroll down the avenue watching the Dboys mobbing in their whips. I choose to stay home. But I secretly want a Dboy, too just not the dusty ones that hang on my block. I want a high roller. But I know what Dboys want.

■■

My virginity is a curse that's chasing me. I'm trying to outrun it. I haven't told anyone, but I want an AIDS test. I see films in Abrahmi's Health class about the deadly transmitted disease and the fear has been gripping me ever since. No one knows about my childhood encounters and they are like monsters hiding under my bed. I feel tarnished like someone has inserted me with venom and it's coming out of my pores. I'm overwhelmed with anxiety. My groin has been hurting since the 6th grade and sometimes the pain is so horrendous that I am paralyzed until it stops. There's a gripping bulge in my vagina that feels like a balloon that swells up with water and I can't move until it dispenses the fluid. I think I have AIDS.

I have test. It's negative. Turns out I have a hernia. She's confused as to why I thought that in the first place. I tell my mom why.

She begs me not to tell my father or my brothers. So, I keep our secret.

8: Forbidden Fruits.

A summer's disregard, a broken bottle top
and a one man's soul[14]

1986. My uncle has three daughters. I lay in their bed drowning in little girls' arms and legs. I've sunk in a sea of blankets and cold feet. I don't know what time it is but through my half-sleep state I feel someone tapping me. I try to brush them off, "Stop Kita." I think one of my cousins is hitting me in her sleep again. The tapping doesn't stop. I roll over taking a large portion of blankets with me as I roll. It's four of us in this bed, me and my uncles three daughters Kita, his oldest, is dark like me and the only one that isn't his biological daughter. The two youngest, Mona and Rea are his splitting image. I am the oldest. We're all tangled in one bed like a game of twister. My mom and his wife Barbara have gone out to the skating rink.

I feel a tug at my arm that snatches me out of my dream and into the madness of covers and sleeping girls. I feel a cold hand on my flesh. I pull the covers from my face and peer into the darkness. I'm startled a bit by my uncle crouched over the bed and reaching into the covers where I lay. His voice is wet and hungry, "You sleep?" I shut my eyes. I think if I lay still enough, he'll go away. Dread washes over me as I remember him twirling me around in his lap when I was younger and how his hands always found the soft spot between my legs. How, even in a room full of adults, he could manage to slither his fingers against my panty line or poke and prod at my private parts.

---

[14] Jackson, Michael. *Man in the Mirror*. Bad. Epic. 1987

46

Tonight, the quietness rings in my ear. The TV he was watching earlier has been turned off. The ceiling fan is loud against the backdrop of stillness. My cousin's rough breathing beside me only assures him that I am alone. *Please God just let him leave.* I try not to swallow as his hands find my soft spot and he taps his drunken rhythm against my private. I roll over; I pretend to change positions in my sleep, closing my legs. I feel his hand on my anus. Disgust rises like a tide in my gut.

I feel his breath in my ear, "Are you woke?" I tense up. I try to appear more sleep than I ever have. I breathe hard like my cousins. He isn't buying it, "You ticklish?" he whispers. He slowly peels the covers from me with the excitement of a hungry man with fruit on his mind ready to peel the skin of an unripe orange. When he frees me from my nest, he slips his hands under me and pulls me to his chest. My uncle, a six-foot-tall man with a husky build, lifts my 11-year-old body easily. I stare at the floor as he carries me over the threshold like a child bride. His room is as dark as a tomb. He lays me in the bed he shares with his wife and hungrily removes my night gown. His eyes are drowsy with lust as he paws my flat chest. He rolls down my Care Bear panties looking at my bare body with desire rumbling from his throat. He lays heavy against my bareness and slides his oily body on mine. Pee is like fire in my belly about to set his sheets in flames. He pushes me to my side. The bed smells sour and funky with sweat and old funky sex, making me queasy. In the darkness, I make out a Michelob beer bottle on the dresser. I hear my mother and his wife earlier saying that he's "Back to drinkin," and I can smell it burning from his breath. I've seen a grown man's penis before but his is massive. My cousin Isiah found a thrill exposing himself to me regularly. I shut my eyes, bury my face in the pillow and lay as still as I can. I had heard him telling my mom that his wife Barbara doesn't satisfy him. She had laughed and said that he should find him someone who does. Now his fleshy penis is rubbing against her daughter from the back and his breathing is getting heavier and heavier. He doesn't enter me but just lays himself against me.

Sweat is dripping from his hairy body like sewage water as he forces himself on me. He's moaning and making grumbling sounds while his fingers are circling between my legs. His meaty belly is bouncing against me. His bristling beard is against my bare back and I feel slob dripping from his lips as he moans a blurry mix of filthy words. He's throbbing and pulsating like a slithering snake that spews sticky venom all over my thin legs and onto his sheets. I lay still as corpse until he's done. I think I even stop breathing as he hisses, "Don't tell anybody about us."

Hush little baby don't say a word.

****

The next day I try to stay invisible. Barbara doesn't seem to notice him watching me; she just stares ahead with fixed eyes. I think she knows because she doesn't look me in my eyes anymore. I guess she can't stand to see the dying of their light. The cartoons we watch on their 19-inch TV now seem as colorless as I feel. She busies herself cleaning and cooking and acts like she can't connect the dots of what's going on in this house. My Aunt, a husky woman with heavy hands and a drooping frown, sits at the sink rigidly hulling peas with her face as hard as asphalt. Her sentences are choppy, "Come eat," "Go play." My cousins are silent too, laughter muted on their lips. They had always been very stand-of-ish. Now the air seems stuffier than it used to be. I wonder if their hearts are pinned to his sleeve like mine.

A few days later Barbara tells me my mom has headed out to California without me. The world stops. She has left without saying goodbye. The walls are coming down around me. I feel like I am on an island and just found out my mother swam to shore without me. I'm drowning because I can't swim in these waters. The rest of the day I walk around with my eyes cloudy like looking through stained glass windows.

I wish the devil was a liar. But the truth keeps coming at me every single night. I lay restless, heart beating out of my chest. The birds and the bees are floating around this house day and night and attack whenever she leaves. I don't know where she goes just that when she's gone, he comes to get me. He's cruising on cocaine freeways now and it's obvious by his sporadic mood swings and sexualized actions. Even red blood between my thighs isn't enough to make him pass over me. He's standing in the doorway with his robe open, nuts hangin. I look away from his big sac. He comes too close. Let's his dick touch my shoulder. He takes me into his room and begins to put his fingers where the sun don't shine. He's hot and wet and the smell of his bed always makes me gag. He's in my ear like, "Yeah you want this dick, don't you?" After he sucks on my breast and taste pieces of me like penny candy, I collect my clothes off the floor and get back in the bed with his daughters with blood on my thighs and underwear. I have nowhere else to go so I hide inside myself.

I wonder why my mom left. I wonder how come she didn't tell me. I know she's not an affectionate woman. Her love is like braille; you got to feel around for it. She's not the kind of person to hold me or tell me she loves me. I just would've thought she'd have said bye. I stay all summer in the yellow house. My spirit is burning to ashes.

Hush, little baby, don't say a word,
Mama's gonna buy you a mockingbird.
And if that mockingbird don't sing,
Mama's gonna buy you a diamond ring

9: Rock, Paper, Scissors. I cover my

insecurities in skin-tight jeans and half shirts. Now that my boyish
gear is replaced by daisy duke shorts and body oil, the boys have
taken notice. Puberty came in with a bang and I feel like a swan
who just realized my fly. I learned to switch my hips to get what I
need. My body is *rockin to the east and rockin to the west* when I
walk. I'm a project chic, a ghetto princess, a bonafied Fly girl. I
look up to the *hussies* and *floozies*. Womenfolk like Sandra on *227*
and Blanche from the *Golden Girls* intrigue me. I like their sexual
power and energy. I take note. I like the confidence and
femininity of Suge Avery in *The Color Purple*. I want to be like her.
I can't be singing Miss Celie's Blues. I'm blessed with a strong
slight build like generations of the corn-fed southern women in
my family. I'm the flesh of my mom's flesh but a meaner more
dominant version. My male friends know I'm beauty with the
beast in my head. I'm crazy and flipped mouth. I took a bat to a
grown neighbor for calling my mom a bitch. I unleashed until Mike
grabbed me and slammed me in the kitchen. Then I took the same
bat to my room and went bananas on my books shelves and
everything else that could come unhinged. Malcolm X and Donald
Goines books were battered on the floor with all the rest of my
things until the riot in my head subsided.

I hate my house. I hate my life. I hate being hungry. I've
always found my way around the emptiness of cabinets in Emery
Glenn and everywhere else we lived. We never had food, so syrup
sandwiches and sugar milk were normal. But it's getting ridiculous
now though. I need a man. I need a hero with superpowers. I

digest Tupac lyrics,

now I'm trapped and want to find my getaway/All I need is a 'G' and somewhere safe to stay.

My mom is all up under the nut sack of a new guy Timothy. I already don't like the dude. From the moment he came he's been barking out orders like he's my father. I guess he really thinks he's my father seein as how I noticed him sporting clothes from the box my dad left behind like he's heir to the throne. He's a skinny nothing ass dude who has brought only a couple garbage bags with him when he moved in a few weeks after I caught my mom and him screwing on the living room floor. It's nothing to me. I've seen her being bodied by three or four Negroes by now. But Tim thinks he runs shit. My mom is smitten like a high school girl in puppy love.

She's in the kitchen making homemade biscuits and eggs with lipstick on. I hear wedding bells. She's been married three times already. I hope this guy isn't husband number 4. I have too many memories of running with her in the middle of the night cause some nigga is kicking our door in. I don't want to run no more. But I can't trust her decisions. I'm trying to figure out how the same man that calls her a bitch whenever he gets mad is the same guy who drives her car all day and has her screaming in ecstasy all night. I see why my dad left. And Tim? He's a loser on every level. She hasn't learned what I already figured out; the yellow brick road doesn't lead to nowhere and there ain't no single moms in fairytales.

My hair is permed now, no more press-n-curls. Now I hit the strip with my Cross-color outfit wearing click of girls and my newest homeboy Suinjata. I met Suinjata making a random crank phone call one night. I hit him with some real sexual shit. I got super filthy with him. I found out his mouth was more gutter than mine.

He was like, "Come on over here and let me lick the lining out that p..." It ended in us talking on the phone all night. I like his nasty ass mouth, but I suspect he's a virgin like me. He goes to Mac High School in West Oakland and calls himself DJ Sin. He's a lanky boy, all head and shoulders. A young boy with old eyes. What I like best about him though is that he loves music, too. He comes to my house to cuff my mom's old *Earth Wind and Fire* and *Gap Band* records so he can use them to DJ his school dance. I don't need them cause I'm into cassettes now. Sin is dirt poor; his clothes are all toe-up. My female friends tolerate his ass cause I like him. Delana's still down with me but our group has expanded to include Amina, my tall home girl who dropped the coke-bottle bifocals and sports dukes like me only she's thicker and built like a woman. I'm in High school now. It seems like every boy is smelling me.

Me and my crew hang over the banisters at Eastmont Mall. We watch Pooh Man and the Luniz perform on make-shift stages and we have competitions to see who can get the most numbers. We all can hit the double digits, but I usually win. Dudes be coming at me like, "Aye let me holla at you." Some Iceberg Slim lookin dude lickin his big lips starring hard at my poked-up ass. He ain't even got a T-shirt under his V-neck sweater. He got on dusty K-Swiss tennis shoes. He cuts to the chase, "Damn let me hit that." *Fuck I look like?*

I give him the business and Amina has a tongue sharper than mine. She hits him with a street-sweeper of curse words, enough to make his head spin. We stand firm like we wish he would run up. We're pretty girls but we can get downright ugly if need be. An older woman coming out of Woolworth shakes her head at us. Amina throws her the finger then slides a rat tail comb in her hair. Don't mistake it; she's ghetto fabulous with her style and dress. We waiting on the bus to take us to Hilltop Mall so we can ride for an hour with no money just to walk around the mall and look cute.

By the time I make it home Tim is on one and my mom is on edge as usual. She's laying still saying she's having another migraine. I think it's a cop out.

Tim is the rat all trifling and sorry
That kissed the mom
That made the money
That paid the bills that fed the kids
That lay in the house my dad built.

He's the big bad wolf breathing nothing but hot air. He's ranting and raving again about us being worthless bitches and my mom not having control of her kids. I guess he forgot he bought my friends a sack of weed earlier. Now we're stupid ass bitches. As usual, my brothers aren't home to witness the tirade. I try to ignore him and pick up the phone and dial Delana's number. Before she can get a "hello" out of her mouth, Tim is standing over me cussing.

He yells "Get your ass off the phone." He starts pointing to the refrigerator talking about us not having any food. He turns to my mom, "You need to have her dumb ass go to the store and get some food for you." Delana's on the other line cussing by now.

I'm still trying to ignore him and figure out what I did wrong, "Hey Delana let me hit you back."

He jumps in front of me, "Hang up the phone before I shove it down your got damn throat."

I lose it. I toss the phone and become belligerent, "Nigga you need to take your lousy ass to the store. You the one who ain't got no damn job you sorry motha-...."

He lunges at me and I swear on God's green earth that I'll have his ass kilt.

I am not my mom. "I ain't Duchess Muthafucka."

He gets so close to my face he's spitting on me, "Bitch I'll kill your ass."

My heart's racing. I'm jumping up and down screaming, "You a bitch and your moms a bitch! You call my mom a bitch every day. So, your mom's a bitch!"

He slams my head back into the wall and before it can go any further my mom jumps between us. I'm going wild.

She's crying and shoving me into the wall, "Nise please stop."

He's yelling and walking around like a caged tiger. She begs me through tears to stop talking. When I don't, she begins slapping me in my face and mouth. I can't calm down. She hitting me and he's calling me every worthless piece of shit name in the book.

My mom is physically strong and by the time she forces me into the stairwell we are both winded and exhausted.

When I catch my breath, I storm upstairs and she makes a run for the doorway to stop him from storming out. I hear her wailing outside giving the neighbors a show. I destroy my room again in a fit of anger. I'm yelling at no one, "Fuck everybody in this house!"

I hit Jay-bird's pager with 9-1-1. He's a 23-year-old green-eyed guy I met on my way to the pay phone when I was 15. He was standing beside the big wheels on his K-5 truck when I strolled by in my jean skort. He was fresh in a crisp white tee and Levi's with a clipped pager on the hip. He asked my name and wrote his pager # down in a hurry. I couldn't believe he was interested in me. The next day on the way to school he rolled up on San Pablo Ave in his money green Corvette and stepped out to hug me like a giant. I could smell Dboy on his expensive cologne. I could see it in his spotless Air Jordan's. He had a couple dope houses in the hood, and I rode my ten-speed to visit him that day. He held my hand while a crackhead screamed at him from a window, "Jay you better leave that lil girl alone." I can page him from time to time and he comes and swings through and pulls me out of the wreckage of my life. He rings back quickly. "What up?"

"Come get me."

"Where you at?" I'm stuffing my bag full of clothes as we

speak.

"At home but I'm going to Delana's"

He hesitates, "I ain't tryna come to the North right now doe."

I had to think fast, "I got something I want to give you."

That's all the motivation he needs.

10: Jbird.

Jamison a.k.a. Jbird is up to the same riga moro as all the guys I know. My Jbird just does it on a larger scale though. He got a pocket full of goals. On top of that, he cut-up and packages dope ass compliments from the moment we met. The boys my age are small time penny-any hustlers serving nickel bags from payphones or a square dude; L 7's singing the ballad of a broke nigga.

My J's a dope dealer and distributes hope by the ounce. He pushes an envy toned Corvette, a money green El Camino with a peanut butter top and a lifted K-5 with 4x4 Monster Truck wheels. He keep bricks in the lining of the door frame of his "under bucket"; a Honda civic, that's the car he drives on 'business' runs. Jbird is a grown man and ain't no love in his stony green eyes but they tell you endless lies of sincerity. He rocks expensive jumpsuits over his powerfully built body.

My Cinder-Ella story begins once upon a Monday morning when he rolls up on me and Sin backpacking it to school at the intersection of San Pablo and Stanford Ave. I cling to his half-empty smile like it's a life raft in my river of hopelessness. He's beautiful. My universe shifts and curves and bends with Jay from the moment we meet. My heart accelerates 60 miles an hour as I lean in the window of his Vette. When he slides me a napkin with his name, "Jbird" written with a ballpoint pen next to his pager number and the #1. I already know what time it is. He breaks it down like a pound, "Hit me up if you ready to fuck with a *real* nigga." Been ready. I'm gone like the wind. Suinjata sighs and feels like bullshit walking beside me in dingy Reebok sneakers. Sin watches the Vette hit the corner and mumbles, "What Jbird supposed to mean anyway?"

Jbird aka Jailbird

Inmate #909348
Age: Approximately 19 to 25 years old
Height: Approximately 6'0" to 6'2"
Weight: Approximately 150 to 170 pounds
Hair: Brown
Eyes: Green
Sex: Male
Race: Black
Scars and Marks: tattoo of a cross on chest
Remarks: The unknown suspect may have a mustache and a light complexion. The suspect typically approaches girls who are alone and on their way to school or work, or are waiting at a bus stop, between the hours of 5:15 AM and 8:00 AM.
Convictions: Possession of narcotics, manufacturing and distribution of narcotics, possession of a firearm, Disorderly conduct, etc.
SHOULD BE CONSIDERED ARMED AND DANGEROUS

His M.O. is easy: smash and grab young girls' hearts.

Tonight, Jay's pushing the K-5 through the bowels of East Oakland, his massive shoulders lean all the way back on his pure white leather throne. His rings glisten from the left hand grippin the woodgrain steering wheel. His chins up like he owns the night.

His outstretched arm sparkles with an icy white gold timepiece. He got a half-empty bottle of Seagram's *Gin*-ocide and orange juice in the cup holder. His big-foot Chevy's turning hoochies heads all down 98th street. The cockpit of the truck smells of testosterone, *Cool Water* cologne and chronic. I'm in the back surrounded by his salivating dog ass friends: Chino, with the dirt under his nails like he just got finished burying a body; and tobacco black Kumar with his yellow eyes feasted on my perky tits. Between a rock and a hard place, literally. I'm balls to nut sack back here. His homeboy, skull-faced Tyrone, rides shotgun like the best man and keeps staring at me through the rearview, undressing me with his eyeballs. Jay's a kingpin who runs the east side and Tye is his side-kick; Batman and Robbin'. Jay smiles at me, lighting me up like a *Black &Mild* cigar. I fake confidence and over-compensate with my smile. I stop kicking my mango sandals and fidgeting like an idiot.

The beat drops some Wu-tang. The deep bass and the smooth treble bubble inside me. Jay looks over his shoulder speaking in the nasal high pitch of Northern Cal guys.

He says, "Roll this up."

My words come out like mumbo jumbo, "I don't... I can't really roll."

The grave diggers laugh. Jay sighs and tosses the sack to Tye. Jay's as blunt as the weed Tyrone rolls, "Let my broad hit that so she can loosen up." I hate myself. We zigzagging through East Oakland. Tye flicks the flame over it and puffs it before passing it back to me. *I don't get high.* I inhale it slow and hold it in like I seen him do. *Be a big girl.* I sip some *Gin* from the styro-foam cup to calm my nerve, but I'm drunk already on Jbird and a fifth of If's. He's sugadaddy sweet. I'm watching him thru his rearview. He winks at me. I drown in him. A bird in the hand is definitely worth more than two in the bush. *A man with a dream with plans to make C.R.E.A.M.* His speakers pumping Wu-Tang clan.
Cash, Rules, Everything, Around, Me
C.R.E.A.M.
Get the money
Dollar, dollar bill y'all-Wu-Tang (C.R.E.A.M.)

<hr>

At G's spot, we climb the stairs of the flat he shares with his mother. My eyes adjust to the light. His mom, a scrawny fiend looking woman with a corn stalk of hair all over her head, is stretched out on his cream-colored couches. As soon as we hit the door, she jumps up and starts cleaning with the quickness. He's snapping at his mom for eating up all *his* food and leaving it in *his* living room. I watch him toss cereal boxes into the trash can. He yells that he's paid for everything in the crib along with the rent. I'm trippin at how everyone treats him like the man of the house. When we pull up at his spots the folks be running around like the pope just arrived. Now here his mother is acting like he runs shit here too. He does; I find out he's the sole breadwinner.

In the room I'm quick to take off my clothes. He lays his gat on the dresser then goes in the bathroom to get high. I don't ask no questions and he don't tell me no lies. I undress down to my pretty zebra print panties; the ones Suinjata tried to convince me not to buy. Tupac's *2pacalypse now* album is in the deck serenading me.

When he comes back, I'm laying on the King size bed's fake satin sheets, back against my elbows trying to look composed but inside I'm shook up. His open closet is full of *Fubu, Karl Kani* and *Polo* gear. His only décor is a big poster of Ice Cube with a pick in his fro. It hits me how much he looks and acts like Amerikkka's most wanted.

He standing there erect in his forest green jogging pants, the rim of his eyes are red. He takes off his *Nike* sweat suit. I stare at his naked body and the cross dangling from his neck like rock candy. His pronounced adam's apple. His emerald green eyes. His body is flawless like a diamond. He has wheat toned skin that's a mix of African descent and the tribe of the red earth people of his Indian Heritage. He got good hair. He reminds me of a lion, a big carnivore with hungry eyes. "take them panties off." I hurry them off. He climbs on the covers and pulls my body to his face by my trembling legs. His tongue feels warm and rough searching thru the tight bushy curls for my clit. He's looking at my face while he licks me with simple brush strokes. I'm soaking wet. He sips me slow like brown liquor. I grab hold of his huge shoulders. My body is pulsating with his tongue. It's not like when my cousin used to swallow me up when I was 5. This feels exciting. My body is tingling about to combust. He flips me over. I feel upside down. My stomach jumps with every brush of his tongue. I put my face in the sheet. My legs around him. I'm too nervous to move so I just lay still as he climbs between my legs and forces them apart with his legs while wiping my sweet juice off his goatee. He sucks my lips with his alcohol drenched breath. I mumble, "You got a condom?" He ignores me. He gives it to me raw; his bare penis is hard, and it tries to enter me strong and forcefully. It's too much pain. He rolls me back over. I grab his arms to brace myself as he pushes into me. It's painful but I squeeze the pain into his back. I fear not being woman enough for him. He's biting his lip as he struggles to penetrate me, "Damn you tight as fuck." *No shit.* I don't want him to know that I'm inexperienced, so I close my eyes and bear the pain, muffling my screams in the hair on his chest while my insides feel like fire. By the time he's in me it feels like the walls have been breached. Hot liquid is sliding down my butt crack. Before long, he's in my skin like a needle, getting me high. His rhythm is powerful and steady. My heart is pounding. I close my eyes and try to ride the beat out. He singing an unchained melody of *ooohhhh ahhhhh.*

His mouth is close to my ear and his breathing is thick and heavy, "You sure you not a virgin gat damn?"

I shake my head no.

Midway in our lovemaking session his mom pops her head in unannounced.

He stops mid stroke and lifts his head with rage burning in his eyes, "Got damn you can't fuckin knock?"

To my amazement she shuts the door quickly. I'm embarrassed but he's too into my body to notice. He grabs my small waist, "You so damn fine." When he cums it's explosive. When he's done, he collapses beside me leaving me wet with his perspiration and dripping his body fluids. The sheets are soaked with cherry red. I have to pee. He rubs my little thigh as he tries to compose himself, "Damn girl, I'm gonna love fuckin you." He's smoldering beside me. Next to him I feel immortal. I look at his body laying naked on top the covers in his room with sticky cum on my thigh. He's absolutely beautiful. He smiles at me, his eyes bright as stars but just as distant. I drown in his attention. He makes me feel like someone. Like I'm visible. I lay my awkward arms around his neck like a herringbone necklace.

I'm gonna love fuckin you too.

11: Mamablackwidow. I hate Tim with a

Passion. We keep bumping heads. The police stay at my house breaking up fights between him and my mom too. When he's not verbally fighting her, he's assaulting me. My mom is not physical. She has the strength of a bull she just timid and doe eyed and will not use it. I will. My brother Mike taught me not to just lay on the ropes and take hits. If he swings at me, I swing back.

Mom lays in the room, curtains drawn blocking out the sun. She doesn't notice me standing in her doorway watching her and listening for words unsung. I want to sit beside her, but I feel unwelcomed. *Mother May I?* Her body has dissolved into a shadow of the military cadet she used to be. Depression has gnawed away her smile and misery is wrinkled in her brow. Reality wore down her laughter. The cellulite on her stomach is a road map back to three c-sections and unplanned pregnancies. She now reminds me of a dried-up raisin in Langston Hughes poem. I can't stand the look on her face; she's all drawn into the gristle with eyes looking colorless and heavy like tears could shake loose at any time. She sleeps half the day and spends the rest somewhere between half-way in-sanity half-way out. So, what happens to a woman whose love has been deferred? If a woman isn't loved, does she dry up like a flower with no water? Does she wrinkle and wither away? I close her door back as I leave her alone with her dreams. The day before, I saw her singing her first tune of the dope-fiend blues. I can't shake the image of her on her knees digging in the trash with bare hands the other day after I accidently threw away a dusty white pill on the coffee table. I shake my head and walk off the sight. I never want to find myself in this dead end of love.

It's my Junior year and this fool Tim hasn't let up. Mike stays at work and my mom sent me and Chettie to Arkansas on the greyhound for the summer. It turns out that she intended on abandoning us again. When I found out that she wasn't sending us our return ticket, I had Jbird wire me the money and hopped my skinny ass on greyhound with the quickness. I won't be left behind again. When I walked into our house my mom quickly cut the cord and told me that I couldn't stay there any longer. *Cool.* I was on my own. I turned in my sandals and headed to Mother Theresa's house. Staying there was two weeks of top ramen and roaches crawling all over me contemplating my next move.

Eventually Krystal, who is now 17 took me in because she's living alone with her brother. She had found her mom unconscious in a pile of her own feces. Turned out she had suffered a major stroke from her drug use and is in a convalescent home. Jbird was in jail, as usual. Her Boyfriend Dlynn is also doing time. Birds of a feather locked up together. I have another job as a waitress at Denny's and I still go to school. I buy my own form fitting, half-shirts and low-cut school clothes and go to school on the first day of school looking like a porn star.
By the time school starts, though, my mom has gone down to the school to tell them I was a runaway. The police force me to return home.

Now I'm climbing the steps at our crumbling apartment in West Oakland by the Acorn projects. Almost all of the city's projects are crammed in West Oakland so it's like a cesspool of violence and drugs.; niggas and roaches. It's an old raggedy dusty old blue building above a Chiropractor Office and across the street from rock bottom; an ancient ruin of a park where fiends get high. We got evicted from the *Condos*. The new place is an old building with a claw tub and high ceilings. I drag my trunk of clothes up the tall wooden staircase with my shorts riding up into my ass, while Tim stands above the stairs mean mugging me. I feel the heat from his stare as I struggle to my small room that's the size of a walk-in closet with a slope ceiling that I can barely stand in. I stare back; double dog daring him to say something.

I stack my cassettes on the dusty sill and read the titles to make sure nobody got me for my goods, Keith Sweat, DJ Quik, RBL Posse, E40. I got a window view of a dope spot where three brothers run drugs and pit bulls. I wave at the youngest brother I've befriended already. I lay on my mattress with my Keds on in headphones blocking out the soundtrack of my mom and Tim arguing about me coming home. Sometimes I just lay awake listening to the gunshots outside my window. But lately I've fallen in love with old soul classic's I found on my mom's cassette mix with Blue Magic's *Sideshow* and The Floaters-*Float on*. I wish I could live in music and words. I curl up next to these songs and feel the lyrics breathing life into me. I want my words to hang in the air like musical notes. It's my coping strategy. It's how I deal with Tim cutting his eyes to the side when I walk by. *Let the Side show begin, hurry hurry, step right on in...*

Tim has declared martial law on me and laid down new rules. I have a strict curfew and though I catch 3 buses to school, or walk if I don't have any change, I still have to make it home by a certain time. I catch the bus in front of the projects at 630am but I'm late to school every day and racking up detentions and Saturday school like it's nothing. A kingpin rides the block watching me from his luxury car. He offers me rides but I decline. My friends aren't allowed to come by. But I've met a neighborhood Muslim kid named Yusef who sits out on the roof with me breaking up bammer weed, listening to DJ Quik's, "Tonight." and talkin crazy shit. *No Stems. No seeds.* He's cool and laid back when he's high though. His scratchy voice always telling me to, "Rewind that junk." DJ Quik is the soundtrack, but the score is the sound of battering rams exploding in the night. We watch police raiding like it's open season on Black youth. We watch tweekers get high and nod off in the park. We watch boys shooting their hopes in netless basketball hoops. We watch the boys next door get dragged out in their drawers by OPD and get stretched out on the lawn like it's hi-def TV. The Police even caught Yusef one night by the BART station, kicked the shit out of him and stuck him in the county.

Jbird gets out of jail and he's like gravity drawing me in on weekends. He's peeped out his rival clockin me and makes plans for me to set him up. He's seen the dealer in his antique Rose Royce hissing at me like a snake, rolling down his illegally tinted windows and trying to slick talk me into kickin it with him. Jay questions me one night while he's blazing some bomb in the driver's side of his Vette and marinates on it, "I be seein ol boy trying to mack you down." I just nod while he continues to plot, "He outta pocket for tryna fuck wit my broad," He stretches out the blunt in his hand for me to hit it, "It's all good. Let him come at you. I'm a ride on his ass." I hit the blunt letting the smoke fill my body. Shit doesn't even matter. I laugh as he plans his attack, "I'm gonna give this nigga the blues." He throws him a surprise party about a week later.

Tonight, I'm on the phone catching Krystal up on my latest rendezvous with the love of my life when Tim scopes me and barges in the kitchen and I'll be god-damned if he doesn't burn holes in me with his eyes again. First, he stands in the door like the boogieman. He's mistaken my phone curfew for earlier than it is. I let him know the correct time. He unleashes on me. He doesn't care what time I thought it was. He doesn't care what my mom has told me. "Get your ass off *my* phone."
Krystal is yelling thru the phone, "Jen just come back to my house." When I live with her, she takes care of me like a mother. At 17 she's only a year older than me but she's way more advanced. She pays bills and writes checks like a grown woman. I'm trying to tell her I'll call her back because Tim's tripping. Before I'm finished, he snatches the phone from my ear and throws it across the kitchen table. By now I'm standing. He's hammering in on me with his long finger in my face, "That's your damn problem now. You think you grown."
I step off a bit.
I'm tired of dude. I yell back, "It's not my curfew time."
He tells me to shut up, "I'll come over there and slap your little ass."

I'm furious, "I wish you would." Tim is small and ugly like a blood sucking insect but he's vicious as a pit-bull, when he gets hold of some bs he keeps it in a death grip. I don't care. I wish any nigga would hit me or disrespect me. I look at him with disgust.
He starts laughing, "What you gonna do?" I flinch. Our voices become more and more amplified. He's like a lion in a cage, "Yeah I'm gonna teach you some respeckt."

My body is an inferno. He yells, "You need to get out my house." He's been spitting venom about my mother letting me come home. He complains that he isn't even raising his own kids how the hell does she expect him to raise hers? I'm tired of him walking around the house ranting and raving like he's on the pulpit and he determines whether or not it's heaven or hell in this house. My mom is stressed out and knee deep in debt. She's started self-medicating and wallowing in pain killers and self-pity leaving me to fight it out with Tim who always seems to keep me in the crosshairs. He comes closer so I can smell the trash in his breath, "What you gone do?" I hope my mom hears. The drugs have her numb and her mind has built fences around what he's says. She just lays around with empty eyes. I don't even know if she hears our shoot-out now. But her silence speaks volumes. Tim's eyes are demon red. I try to warn him, "Don't hit me!" He takes it as a threat and lunges toward me. It's like he pulls a trigger. I go up in emotional flames.

Before his hand can land against my cheek, I grab a cast iron skillet from the table and swing it with all my might. He recoils and the pot barely misses connecting with his head but bangs against his arm and finally the wall. He's hot as fish grease now,
"Bitch you tried to hit me?"
I use the pan as a weapon to keep distance between us. I swing madly. If he comes near me, I'm going to beat his brains out. I know I am. He's yelling that I am going to die tonight. I'm dodging his hands and his words like shrapnel and debris.

"You stupid little bitch." *I know you are but what am I?*
And then he catches me. He grabs me with both hands and pushes me toward the window. He's too strong. I catch myself in the frame as the window breaks and shards of glass bust out onto the street two-stories below us.

He bangs the pan out of my grip. By now my mom is rushing in in a panic. He's trying to grab me and force me through the window but I'm swinging at him with everything I have. He's ponding on my arms. I don't have the pan anymore, so I throw hands.

My mom grabs him, "Stop, stop hitting her!"

He's out of control, spitting like a rabid dog and screaming, "Bitch I'm gonna throw you out this fuckin window and come out there and stomp your bloody body into the ground!"

He doesn't realize the neighborhood boys have heard the commotion and are gathering like hyenas. I flip out and go berserk throwing shit in the kitchen. I'm chunking dishes and flipping over chairs. My mom is frantic trying to keep us apart. He tells her he is going to leave her, and she becomes distraught.

Men leave.

She doesn't get it yet.

It's the same ole game.

Now she's running down the long hall begging him while I am left in the kitchen almost hyperventilating.

When she returns, I can see it in her eyes. She hates me.

She's frantic, "Denise you have to leave."

I'm in disbelief. My voice cracks, "He tried to hit me first!"

She has a look of doubt on her face, "I don't believe that he'd do that. Are you sure? I told you about your attitude problem."

I'm stunned into silence. Her words have me in a choke hold. She is trying to get me to agree that Tim didn't hit me. She wants me to say that he never hit me. I can't agree. She doesn't want me to call the police. She begs, "Just go." I grab my shit. I damn near knock her down as I leave. It kills me how weak she is.

I climb down the stairs weak and weary from the altercation. Outside the boys on the block draw closer to me like a swarm of bees. That one guy who asked me for 25 cents to make a call one day. That dude I told to watch his ass cause the cops were running his name thru the block. Old boy who has taken me to Oakland coliseum to watch games and smoke weed is leading the pack, "What the fuck, ma?"

By now I'm crying, "My mom's boyfriend is trippin again." It's easier than having to explain. *This old man he played one, he played knick knack on my thumb...*

The corner boys mobilize without saying much but I know it's on. Ready to rock n roll.

Tension gripping in their fist.

The wrath of young black anger bubbling in their faces.

I wave them back. "It's all good."

But they want to get at him so bad it's eating at them, "You know we'll serve that fool."

They are hot blooded young goons who get life from violence. I resist the urge to have the guerilla's beat the brakes off Tim. Instead I sit on my trunk full of clothes on the curb thinking of a master plan, "*cause ain't nuthin but sweat inside my hand.*"- Rakim

My stomach turns in knots. *Now where the hell am I gonna go?*

One of the dudes, Maniac, pulls up in his Deuce and a Quarter and offers me a ride to Krystal's house. He pulls out a sack of weed. I partake. He tells me that that he's gonna meet Tim in the back yard in a ski-mask. I shrug and get out the car. I stand in Krystal's door with a buck and a prayer. She opens the door as usual.

But now Dlynn is there. Now that he's out of prison the roles have reversed and she's supporting him on the welfare she draws for her brother. Her mother is still in recovery and has lost all her motor skills. I'm just another mouth to feed. When $20 comes up missing I feel the unspoken accusations. I steal but I don't steal from friends. I'm like the spook who sat by the door when I hear Dlynn whispering to Krystal, "That bitch probably got it."

He has no idea of the bitch I am beginning to become.

12: The Come up is a necessary evil in the hood. Everybody got a hustle. There's a rhythm to poverty; a rise and fall, a beat that everything dances to: the timing of the mail man slipping the checks into the mailbox on the 1st and 15th. The flow of merchandise from booster to street vendor to home. Repeat. The pattern of serving dope fiends from the corner to the stash on the side of abandoned houses. The song of the police sirens. The *click clack* of the ten-speed bike pedaled by a Jordan wearing toy soldier collecting hood intel. We get comfortable with this tempo. We're just keeping time though. We forget that there's always a down beat, that everything moves, vibrates and circles back. That everything has an opposite. This the time when the pendulum swings backwards. Sin calls it *funk mode*--when shit is all jacked up. It's a melancholy tune of the how long blues; eviction notices, empty fridges, boys suspended in time behind bars. For me it's the sobering realization that I can't come up. That it doesn't matter how much I beg, borrow or steal, I'm still broke as hell. I can't win for losing.

I been window shopping at the Gap on Broadway for too long. I blow in with my red 49rs Starter coat like little red riding-hood cruising the aisles. There's a sign that reads *Boot-cut jeans on Sale for 39.99*. I ain't got no money but I'm browsing the jean section for my size ir-regardless. I hold a pair up to me like I'm confused about my fit. I grab three pair. I'm flipping through colorful tank tops on the table, keeping my eyes on the gear. I can feel the salesperson keeping me under heavy surveillance. I peep a camera by the register out of my peripheral. I know not to look up. I haunted several stores by now. I know this dance. A salesman approaches me, "Can I help you?" I light him with a 100-caliber smile, "I'm just looking." Dude smiles back through barb-wired teeth. I'm all over the place and he's keeping up in his lug boots and khaki pants. I grab the jeans, two red tanks, the black and yellow socks. I swerve past him with an armful of merchandise and head to the dressing room. He's too busy smiling. He's talking at me through the door, "Let me know if you need another fit baby doll."

I send him off on a wild goose for a size 5 while rolling up my size 2 and stuffing it inside the lining of my coat. I slide in a couple shirts and smooth it out before zipping it.

I toss a handful of clothes to him as I leave.

"These didn't work out."

He's looking concerned, "Can I get you another pair?" he asks.

"Nope."

I proceed to the exit. When I cross the threshold the metal detector shrieks. I halt. We're both at a stand-off for a second, both looking confused. I'm weighing my options. Do I bow out gracefully? *Naw-never that.* But I think if I run, he'll probably catch me. Do I beg for mercy? *Shit naw.* I stand my ground, shrug my shoulders.

He slow walks to me, "Remove your coat please."

I smirk and slide my arms out of my coat, holding it up like *what?* I pull out the coat pockets like I'm irritated. I shake the coat and turn around letting him scope my perky tits in my tank top and butt cheek hanging out my shorts, "I ain't got nothing." I'm a bold-faced lie. The truth ain't in me.

He tells me to walk back through. The shit goes off again. He looks at my open coat and doesn't see anything. I don't have pockets on me. He can't figure it out. I look annoyed like he's wasting my time. He stands there for a moment and folds his arms across his chest. I raise my brows, "Can I go?"

He squints at me like he isn't quite sure. Then looks over his shoulder at the other salesperson, "yeah, you good."

I fold my coat in my arm and step off with the alarm blaring. Sweats rolling from my arm pits. Outside I hit the block in breakneck speed.

13: Amerikkka's nightmare is my

dream man. He loves me. He loves me not.

For Jay, love is mathematics; just facts and calculated steps and shit I can't figure out. I'm not good at math. So, I find myself losing count. Minutes, and hours and days crumble into fractions of time he spends with me. He packs me tight between hustles like weed in his swisher sweet. I get half empty smiles, mixed messages, X's and O's, and shit like that, minus his heart.

Suddenly things don't add up anymore. This love thing has become the sum of all my fears. I look in the mirror and see my mother's face. I'm tired of collecting pieces of him. Things like phones calls and visits and counting money are measurable moments but when that stops it becomes problematic. I can't seem to make any sense of this love thing. Good thing love ain't logical. He can still count on me. I'm a ride or die chick

Jbird totes his gun in his waistband. But his anger is a concealed weapon. He yanks me by my ponytail. He drags me from his car kicking and screaming onto the asphalt. Barely answers my pages. Just like that-- Things fall apart. I'm finding cut up straws with blood on the tips in his car and when I question him, he goes blazing mad. I know something isn't quite right. He nods off in traffic at a stop light. I look over at him and he's slumped in the driver's seat napping. I shake him awake. He pops up and starts driving erratic. Even during sex, I notice his stillness, pull his head up and he's dozing. He's moody and mean. One minute the sun is shining on us, the next it's the coldest winter ever. He knocks holes in the wall with his fist and threatens to kill me because of insane thoughts he has about me messing around with other guys. The thought of me sleeping with someone else is tormenting him. Yeah, the honeymoon been over. Our love is like war now. I can deal with his constant jail time. I can even deal with his drug dealing. But it's the flashing that has me on edge and the fact that he always stays strapped.

He's paranoid, toting a gun on his waist inside the house. We get in the car and he's driving reckless to lose an invisible tail. I strain to see out the side mirror. There's no one. He yanks the car to the side of the road and shuts his lights off. I'm watching his rapid eye movements. I imagine the enemy is guilt and it's coming for his soul. His temper is paper thin and I'm walking on eggshells daily. Yeah, the sky is falling. But in my mind, I'm still down. *Down down baby, down down the roller coaster. Sweet, sweet baby I'll never let you go.*

■■

We're basking in the wet heat of post sex and he's wiping his balls with a hand towel. He's talking business on the phone planning robberies with someone. It sounds like they plan on holding up a bank. I know he's a jacker; a kick door burglar at best, but I don't know the extent of his crimes. I'm shocked that he needs a whole crew. He's pacing and talking, *"Yeah* I need you and Dee to go in first. Pete can stay in the car. I'll go over the counter. Tell Big not to get the car till the day we doin the shit yada yada" I seen him run up on a dude all by his lonely. What kind of dirt is he planning where he has to have a driver and a look-out?

This is emotional suicide. I love someone I don't know. I'm listening to him talk. I'm laying across his bed with the salty after taste from giving him head for the first-time tart in my mouth. I can't believe I suck dick now. He storms up to me, eyes blood shot and white powder on his nose. He's telling me to get dressed, 'I'm taking you home." I get up reluctantly and search for my jean skirt wondering what I did this time. I mumble some shit like, "I hate you sometimes." This infuriates him. He grabs his pistol from the dresser and points it at me. I freeze in my bra and panties. I'm stone still. His face is unrecognizable in its fury. He lowers the gun and steps in my face, "You hate me?" I can't speak. He holds the gun handle out to me with his nostrils flared. I don't want it but I'm afraid to leave it in his hand. I take it with trembling hands.

73

The gun is heavier than I imagined. He has a weird smirk on his face, "If you hate me, shoot me." I try to say something, but my words dry up in my mouth. He starts yelling and pounding on his chest like King Kong, "Shoot me then." I'm in a ball of confusion. He yells, "Pull the trigger." If I lift the gun will he overpower me? If I give it back will he shoot me? He's commanding me to shoot him. I wince. I picture myself blowing his brains out and them splattering against his closet door. Why is he doing this? I lower my eyes. I whisper in a barely audible voice, "I don't want to shoot you." I'm shaking like a leaf when he reaches down and snatches the gun from me, "Then shut the fuck up." I catch his drift and sit back on his bed. He's decides not to take me home. He laughs as an after-thought, "The gun was empty anyway." I start crying. I feel like my superman is turning into a villain. I'm often ambushed by crazy accusations and power trips. Everyday he's playing ping-pong with my emotions. One minute I'm screaming his name, the next I'm screaming from fear. One day I order a child's happy meal and he grabs the bag and tosses it out the window before telling me to "Grow the fuck up." I just turned 17.

I'm his leading lady now it seems but I still feel like a little girl. He picks me up from school on a regular now. He doesn't have a lot of time because he's on the block like clockwork, but he doesn't post up like most of the boys my age. He runs dope houses and moves weight. He sells Heroin as far as I know. He's getting more and more paranoid, but he says I'm his angel. He says God won't let nothing happen to him as long as I'm with him, so he keeps me next to him now while he does his dirt. He feels like people want to kill him, "But they ain't gonna catch me slippin. I got some heat for these niggas." He's always watching over his shoulder, but I realize that it's personal demons he's really running from. I just don't know what they are.

Day by day it's more impossible to cope
I feel like I'm the one that's doing dope...- Geto Boys (Mind playin
tricks on me)

We pull up at one of his houses and the females go crazy when they see the Corvette. *All the lil girls on J-bird street love to hear the robin go tweet, tweet, tweet, rockin robin.* Even the males run out to the car damn near opening his car door for him. I follow him inside and sit on the rusty orange couch. There's a pretty brown skinned chick and a white girl all in Jbird's face. I kind of like the way they treat him like he's the man, my own Dr. feel good.

Before long everyone disappears leaving me alone on the couch watching an episode of Martin trying not to laugh too loud when I hear commotion in the back. The white girl runs out in a panic with blood on her shirt yelling in high frequency, "Oh shit, oh shit." She has a cordless phone in her hands. "Call an ambulance." I'm sitting on the couch looking stuck on stupid. The girl is shaking. Her hands are bloody, and she got pixie dust on her nose. Jbird runs in to calm her down. He grabs the phone from her, "Chill out." The girl is hysterical. She's flipping out. But Jbird motions her back into the back. I stand up and walk slowly to the hallway and what I see almost makes my knees buckle. I see the brown girl laying on the floor in the bathroom with her nose bursting with blood. Blood is in the toilet. Blood is on the floor. It looks like her eyes are rolling in the back of her head. One guy is slapping her face and shaking her limp body. Jbird steps over her, closes the door and rushes out. He's pushing me back down the hall, "Go sit down." I lose my head and start yelling, "What happened to her?" He yells over his shoulder, "Nothing. Go sit down." I sit down. I'm starting to shake. By the time we are cruising down McArthur in his Vette he explains to me that she was snorting hop and it went bad. I'm tripping. His nose starts bleeding and I get a sinking feeling.

14: Nowhere

Amina unscrews the cap on some Seagram's and pours it into some orange juice in a Styrofoam cup. We rollin down the street on the bus sippin on Gin and Juice...laid back. I know I'm fly in my red bra-top, cut-up jeans and dookie braids with my neon Motorola pager on my hip looking like a video vixen. We damn near stop traffic at the bus stop and there's a chorus of "Aye baby" "Aye baby" We're three deep. Amina and Delana are with me now on the 72 headed downtown.

Tia is on punishment and can't come. Suinjata's gonna meet us when he gets his gear together and take off those crazy Zupa wild print pants he had on looking like the Fresh prince Of Bel-Air. He's kind of scrubbish and Delana and them are irritated that I'm letting him tag along. She staring at me hard through her bright colored *stay-high* glasses when I tell her my homeboys coming. She's popping bubble gum while she talks, smacking her glossy lips, "Fuck it. I don't care. It's gonna be hella fun tonight." She's Miss Mary Mack all dressed in black spandex. I'm giddy cause I know it's gonna be so many boys packed into the two-story building. Amina is combing her silky *Dark & Lovely* perm like, "Hell yeah, they gonna be jockin me tonight." She ain't lying either. She got on her shorts from Durant Square flea market, lumber-jack shirt and wheat color Timberland boots cleaned with a pencil eraser. We're going to the Boys Club. It's in the heart of downtown so the party will be beating with guys from all four corners of Oakland. It's going to be lovely.

We jump off the bus delighted to see the crowd already winding around the side of the building. The air is thick with teenage hormones raging. Rough necks are yelling our way from rag top Chevy's and drop Impalas and trying to pull over to the curb. It's a feeding frenzy. Guys are like:

"Damn you hella thick,"

"Aye Baby let me talk to you for a minute."

We smile, rump shaking, and waving like local celebrities. None of the girls here can fade us. I peep ball caps with sets from WSO, B-Town, C.R.E.W., and I get excited. *Boo-yah!*

It's on. We're feeling ourselves in the party. I'm in motion on the dance floor jamming to Dr. Dre's Nuthin but a G thang. *It's like this and like that and like this and uh.* The floor packed with youngsters, the air heavy with dank smoke. Bodies are rocking and bumping up into me. I'm shaking what my mama gave me. It's dudes from Hayward, Richmond and even Vallejo in the house popping their collars. There's body rolling freaks with air brushed faces. Young East Bay gangsters are getting rowdy but we ain't sweating it. The 808 is kicking bass through my blood. I'm bumping and grinding with a fine dude in Eddie Baur jeans, putting my hands on my hips letting my backbone shake.

I see Tia's brother, Jamel, in banana yellow Cross-Colors gigging on Amina's booty. Her rump is shaking like a tambourine. We start jamming to Wu-Tang "Bring the Ruckus" when dudes start throwing up sets. The DJ yells to represent where they are from and it's like throwing a match into a powder keg. The room explodes in gang signs and chants. It's dark so we can barely tell when a fight breaks out in the corner. We just see hands flying and the crowd is pushing back. I tug on Delana who is posted on the wall talking to a guy with finger waves in his hair and a link chain swinging from his neck, "They fighting." Delana ain't too worried and shrugs me off, "It's not that serious." She got Seagram's Gin flooding thru her veins and her mind is just like her kitchen styled hair-warped by the heat.

Then the crowd goes wild. Pockets of fights break out all

over the dance floor. By now me and Amina are huddled near the wall with Delana trying to dodge the swinging crowd. It's too dark. Bottles are smashing. Girls are screaming and guys are shouting in the dark, "Aye turn on the lights!" No one can see. The DJ is still spinning records and the lights are still out. It's chaos. I'm getting more nervous. I can't tell which way the fights are. Delana's shook now too. She yells, "let's bounce." I'm in agreeance. We make our way to the exits steering clear of the growing mass of boys fighting. I'm unprepared for what I see. In the hall it's straight mayhem. Everything is upside down. The fight has spilled to the hallway and onto the stairs. I look over the balcony and see boys falling into the tables and others swinging and kicking at rivals. They're fighting on the banisters. They're fighting by the bathrooms. A girl gets punched out trying to protect her boyfriend from a mob of boys who are stomping him by the fountain. We look at the stairs and see security trying to round up boys and stop them from leaving.

They yell to other guards to lock the doors. One boy breaks from the crowd and yells up the stairway, "I'm killing everybody in this muthfucka!" *Everyone?* My mouth gets dry. Delana's eyes look just as panicked as I know mine do. Amina is gripping my shoulder tight, acrylic nails digging into my shoulders. We turn as pistols start popping and echoing in the building like firecrackers. I'm running in a circle like a trapped mouse not knowing which way to turn. We hear other shots. Suddenly it's a warzone. I zoom in on a window and see boys climbing through it. I run full speed and hit the window, but I pump the brakes on the ledge. Boys are flying past me jumping and falling into the construction that's attached to the building. Delana runs up behind me and pulls me back, "Jen don't." I'm scared. All I can think about is escape. My heart is beating in my chest. But Delana is adamant, "They probably shooting at them." It makes sense. I run slipping and shit to the janitors closet where Amina is already stuffing herself in. It's packed with big eyed girls. Me and Delana squeeze in and huddle with them. The gunshots sound like they will never end. I can hear girls whimpering and shuddering with each blast. Someone unleashes a semi-automatic outside. *What kind of weapons do they have?* I close my eyes and jump in place with my arms wrapped around my little body. *Please God let me live.*

Then it stops. It's like we all have been holding our breaths and when it stops, we exhale. My heart stabilizes. We stand there forever it seems just breathing and waiting. One girl finally opens the door a crack and peeks out. The dance floor is empty. The lights are on now. We are tip toeing across the wooden floor side-stepping hats and torn pieces of clothing. We survey the hall and see others fleeing the building. We climb the stairs sideways on wobbly legs and make our way to the lobby. There's blood on the floor and people are crammed in the door trying to all squeeze through at once. I am too ready to breath the fresh air outside.

We rush at the doorway like bats flying out of hell. I push and pull my way through the crowd losing sight of Delana and Amina out of my eagerness to get of the building. I realize as I'm jumping into the crowd, what's stopping the door up. Boys bodies are laying in the doorframe. I'm still too panicked to stop so I'm stepping over them like everyone else. I have my hand on the frame and I'm pulling myself into the doorway when I see yellow pants. I freeze. Time stops. My mind is trying to collect my thoughts. But I can't quite wrap my mind around it. *Who had on yellow Cross Colors?* I can't jog my memory. I'm too scared to think. But my mind is pulling me back to the dance floor. *Jamel!* Oh No. I crumble where I'm standing. Tia's brother Jamel is one of the boys laying in the doorway. His abdomen is opened up like a gutted fish belly. His friend, Tony, with blood-soaked clothes is trying to pull him in through the mass of people who are stepping on his friend as they leave. There are other boys throwing brown paper towels on the victims to stop the bleeding.

People are yelling that some kids are snatching shoes and jewelry off the wounded. I crawl out onto the floor on all fours and get up out the club then look around for my friends. When I see Delana and Amina I know they have seen him too. Delana's

crying. I can hear Jamel screaming from excruciating pain. He got blood in his nose and in the corners of his mouth. It's gut-wrenching the way he's screaming. I never heard a voice that high pitched. People are dipping out, running fast down the stairs. Kids who have finally made their way out of the building are laughing, "Damn these dudes got smoked."
Cars are burning rubber, peeling off.

I take off running down the stairs and down the street. Delana and Amina have jumped off the porch and are running behind me. All I can think is that we need help. *He's gonna die. He's gonna die.* I make it to the payphone on the corner and snatch the phone and rapidly dial Tia's number. As soon as I hear his mother's sleep drenched voice, I blurt out, "Jamel got shot! We need help!" The phone drops. I'm yelling into the phone, "Hello?" It's a few seconds before I hear Tia's voice in the phone. I can hear her mom shrieking in the background. She's distraught. I'm trying to explain to Tia, "He's been shot. I think in the chest. Oh my God." Delana's screaming beside me, "Oh my God he's dying!" Tia is taking directions. They make it to the scene before the ambulance arrives.

The night ends with me and my friends packed into Tony's car who's fresh out the county jail and has no license. He's like a mad man with blood still fresh on his shirt mobbing through the steep inclines of Oakland's hills to Highland Hospital swearing death on the niggas who did this to his *lil homie.* We in the emergency room and his eyes are ominous dark clouds. I know it's on.

It seems like everyone is getting shot. The little dude I tutor name Kilo gets killed. Delana's brother catches heat his graduation night when he and a few friends attempt to rob someone. It's becoming a common occurrence, *guess who got shot?*

I write a poem about my life titled, "Nowhere," on a slip of paper and Delana finds it. It's just some rambling about how hard it is in Oakland and that I feel like I am going nowhere. She gives it to Shep, and he publishes it in the school paper. I'm embarrassed and mad at Delana. The whole school is buzzing about it and Shep even gives me a nod of approval. He says that I can write well. I have a way with words. I just have so much pent up frustrations and that sheet of paper I wrote on was a just a release.

Nowhere

I feel like I'm in a cold dark place
Full of so much hurt and so much rage
My face is blank like this page
I'm going nowhere, just running in place
In a black hole with no escape
Every day is just like yesterday
Another ordinary empty day
I'm just here
Taking up space
I'm nothing special
Not exceptional in any way
And I don't care
I feel like nothing
no place
and I'm going nowhere

15: **P**oor **Righteous Teacher.**

My Spanish teacher, Mr. Burris is an elderly black man who wears 1970's polyester leisure suits. We take him as a joke. I don't know if he even hablo español. He always picks me out in class to read and answer questions. I have enough sense to memorize the passages in English and read them back like I know Spanish so it's an easy A for me. He'd much rather give us a sermon about life than teach Spanish anyway. Today he's paying tribute to the many friends we have lost. I think he has dementia. He always goes on and on about evil and how the world is going to self-destruct. I can't stand this dude.

Today he's on one. A dude name Chill is trying to smile at me. My fat Gucci Braids hang down my back like the snake-headed creature Medusa and I got an expression so stone cold it's an ego killer. I'm scribbling on my red notebook, *J-Bird* and circling his name with a universe of hearts. Burris is ranting and raving to us about being Black in America, like we don't know. He's standing at the front by the chalk board with sweat marks on the armpits of his button-down shirt wiping his forehead with a handkerchief as he reads us our eulogy, "Every last one of yall will be dead before you turn 18. You keep living like you do! I been here at this school twenty years and done went to more funerals. If this is how you want to live, then I give you my blessing" I roll my eyes. We are on notice. We are bored with his preaching. He doesn't care.

He continues, "None of you will live to see 25. I can guarantee you that! And I'll preach at your funerals. Consider yourself lucky if you go to jail." Burris is out of breath after he gives us a fire and brimstone sermon that MLK couldn't fuck with. I shrug. No big deal. I don't think I'll be alive at 25 anyway. Through the window I see Jbird's shiny tires rolling into a parking space. Dope-boy Fresh. The bell rings and I throw my home girls the deuces. Free school lunch taste too bitter to me and school seems ridiculous. I won't be making it to the rest of my classes. Mr. Burris stops me at the door, "I thought you'd be the most likely to succeed young lady."
This nerdy guy named Charles spits over his shoulder, "Most likely to be a prostitute." It feels like a sucker punch. *Stick and move.* I look down at my skintight designer jeans and half shirt with my exposed belly and bust back, "Fuck you," then set him on fire with my glare.
Do what's best and walk away. I smirk. *I got a full clip patna.* Mr. Burris looks saddened. Sorry to disrespect a teacher who thinks so highly of me. I'm the wrong bitch to fuck with, though.

16: Tha Crossroads.

It never rains in Southern California, but it's been pouring down for like a month in Oakland. Even Jesus can't help but weep. Chuck Taylors and Jordan's skirt every inch of the pews. The wood panel walls of the church are framed with head-bowing teenagers and the air is unstable with combustible black rage.

Tracy's funeral came out of nowhere. Shell-shocked teenage boys are pallbearers; niggas with attitudes, carrying the burden of truth. His cousin Irah is fighting mad, jaw tight like the gunfire still echoes in his head. This day our emotions are like rivers flowing away from its source--unnatural. I can hear a harmony of sniffles from young men with retribution in their gaze. The around-the-way-girls whimper with mascara tear streaked faces and heads bowed like wilted roses. The organ weeps while a singer buries him in music, "His eye is on the Sparrrrow." I'm stone faced, gravely silent, looking at my classmate Tracy in the casket. He's frozen like a picture, suspended in time; forever young. Sweet 16.

It's like a class reunion in here. I'm looking at people I hadn't seen in a minute. Dropouts, Dope boys, and nerds. Keisha's sitting with a big belly wiping tears. I hadn't seen her since she tried to kill herself by drinking a bottle of rubbing alcohol in the 8th grade. Her father had checked out in her backyard-blowing his brains out on the vinyl seat in his Oldsmobile. She looks good. Her vocal cords gone, though. I see Jamani with blood shot eyes standing beside Tone who's still wearing crutches from a hit and run accident he was in. I'm glad Melvin is out of jail now. I see all my teachers and school staff with the same old expressions they always hold at funerals. I try to focus on Mr. Burris delivering tribute in the wake of Tracy's murder. I came to pay my respects. I have loving memories of Tracey; a good boy sitting hunched shouldered in class taking notes. He was gunned down coming from playing basketball with his cousin. It had to be a mistaken identity because Tracy never had a problem with no one.

You never feel more alive than you are sitting at a funeral of someone your age. I flinch when I hear the wailing coming from the back of the church and I'm scared to look back. Tracy's mom can't even make it into the church without collapsing in agony. It's a gut-wrenching long howling sound that could shatter the stained-glass windows. Pain grips me by the throat and almost stops me from breathing. When I look back, her brothers are carrying her, twisting and screaming from the building, "Why they do that to myyyyyy son. Oh, Gawwwwwd whyyyyyy." I gasp like I been holding my breath. Delana squeezes my hand, her face contorted with the ugliness of grief. Ain't no watered-down gospel coming from Burris this time. This eulogy is already written. He composes each tear and sniffle, every sound and every voice. He pleads for a cease fire, "Stop this killing!" every heart says Amen. His voice has a new fury to it, "We can't keep burying our children! Death is stalking our young men! If you want to live stand up." Next thing I know tennis shoes are on the ground. 500 faces with no tomorrows. I'm standing in my sandals; my tears are relentless raindrops. His mother's sorrow is thundering in my head.

I stand outside watching a constellation of ragtops, big-bodies and low riders parade off with the Limo carrying Tracy's casket. I think about all the classmates I've lost lately. Mike's friend Majado gets shot in the face with a sawed-off shotgun after someone puts 187 in his pager. Death is an inferno that seems to be swallowing everyone I know; Kilo- the boy I used to tutor, Robin, Pretty faced Rico, and Keith, just a bunch of abbreviated lives. It's like a bomb has gone off and we are the surviving strong left in the fallout. I'm unraveling in this madness, dying vicariously through others. Every week is filled with grave stories of dead boys and empty spaces. Tone, Bell, Frick, all souls on ice. My classmate Joran's standing vigil outside smoking a square on the broken sidewalk. He hugs me, "I can't believe Tracy's gone." No one says anything. The truth is buried 6 ft deep in our chest. He's got one Jordan in the grave. He speeds off following the procession of cars with Tupac playing on the system in his Eclipse like a battle war cry. He dies a few days later. Ashes to ashes, dust to dust.

17: REDBULL.

I guess Misery loves company cause Jbird keeps picking me up just to fuss with me. I'm working at Ross clothing store now, stealing him all kinds of shit. I have a hole cut in the liner of my new coat and ripped out insides. Shit I can stuff whole outfits in this one. I hit them for leather gloves and hats in the winter. I even wear raggedy shoes and slip into a new pair before the day is out. I'll go the dressing room and slip clothes on under my work clothes. Hell, I even left out with about ten pair of panties on one day under my skirt. I don't give a shit.

By now I'm spending more time with Suinjata and that's a point of contention for Jbird. Suinjata's a kid like me but he has paternal instincts like my brother Mike. I guess that's why I like having him around. He take care of me. He's a voice of reason in my irrational world. His sole mission in life is spinning records and following me around. He was at my house the first time that Jbird came to visit so he thought he was my brother. But now it's a problem. I don't see the threat. Suinjata is a skateboarding boy who lives in a studio apartment with his artist mother and dresses like a skateboarder. He hustles change in the parking lot at the grocery store for loadin ole ladies' groceries. Half the time, I feed him. He gets his money like Mike, straight elbow grease. His only legit come up is that he DJ's the school dances. He's a hell of a DJ so his popularity around town has been on the rise.

Suinjata saves up enough money to buy a small Toyota and fills it with crates of old school records. He's always talking to me about this party and that party. I don't think anything about having him drop me off at Jbird's crib. He's bumping his gums trying to get me to help him come up with some money to host a Jamboree with the rapper Tupac as a performer. I don't believe he can pull it off. He's begging me, "Talk to Jay and see if he can front me some money."

"He ain't gonna do it."

I've rode the bus from downtown to 125th where Jbird stays on many of days and he hasn't had an issue with that. But when he sees the red truck, Jay runs out like a raving bull and snatches Suinjata from the driver's seat. Suinjata is scared as hell. Jay bird's breathing fire, "Who is this nigga?" I'm holding Jay's arm and begging him to stop and his fury turns on me. I beg Suinjata to please, drive off. Upstairs in his room Jbird is pounding his fist into the wall damn near beating a hole into it yelling, "I'll kill yo ass." I'm trembling. I know he will. I can see it in the cold fire of his eyes. I try to tell him that Suinjata only came to get me because he left me stranded at work, again. I tell him Suinjata wants him to invest. This enrages him. He slaps me so hard across my face and ice water runs through my veins. I damn near stop breathing. It takes me off guard. Not that he hit me, but the sting of shame comes from not fighting back. I'm Jenni-boe. I fought niggas all my life. He leans into me using the wall to brace himself, "If you bring that nigga back to my house, I'll kill you and him." His mom is starring big eyed as I make my way down the stairs behind him, my vision blurry with tears. He throws me the keys to his car. "Get me to the spot." I see powdery crumbly substance and straws with burn marks in the ashtray.

I can't drive. My legs are like jello when I start the car up and try to maneuver it out of its parking space. I'm afraid of what he will do if I wreck. I know the basics but not enough to drive him where he needs to go. He insults me and drags me out of the car onto the street and assassinates me with words, "You dumb ass bitch." I find my way to the passenger side. At the dope spot everyone's catering to him again, the dope man. He's barking orders out and suddenly turns to me. His eyes soften, "Give me a massage." I rub his back without question. While I'm trying to will the shake from my hands, I realize my deepest fear- That one day I'd look in the mirror and see my mother's face. I knew better than to fall in love. I was a fighter who had surrendered my mind and body to a man. I'm a rose trapped in his heart of concrete.

But what he doesn't know is that I was born between a rock and a hard place. When I'm wounded and hurt, I find a way to break free.

Our relationship is exhausting. I'm almost happy when he goes back to jail.

18: The Breaks.

Shit is getting real. Jbird is on a long stint in jail but I'm knee deep in this love thing. I want to be a down ass bitch; a ride or die type of chick so I continue to send my letters to the penitentiary. I've moved back home now. I'm way down on my luck. I don't tell my friends, but I am living in an almost empty house with no utilities and no food. Rock bottom.

My mom has slowly but surely moved out and into Tim's new place. Tim had decided he'd had enough of playing father and moved out. I would hear my mom begging him to come home. Then she disappeared. It started with me coming home and finding little odds and ends missing and then it was the floor model TV and everything else of value. Then one day I noticed her closet was as empty as the refrigerator and I kicked her closet door closed in anger. The bills are in my name and they started calling me relentlessly. When I couldn't hold the bill collectors off any longer, the shut off notices turned into disconnections and that turned into darkness. Every day I wake up it's like opening my eyes in hell. I keep a candle and matches at the bottom of the stairs to light my way around the dark house when I get home. I'm just riding out the storm. Usually I just try to stay gone. My brother Mike does the same. He's met a girl who lives in Vallejo and he camps out at her and her mom's crib. It's every man for themselves now. Suinjata throws the most epic party in the Henry J. Kaiser and Tupac performs. He tells me later that he found a dealer to invest. Now he has been accepted to UC Irvine on a full scholarship. I don't even tell him the hell I'm going through when he shows me his acceptance letter. I'm happy for him.

I toss and turn in the dark with my stomach retching and throwing up pink frothy liquid from the horse pills I have to take for Chlamydia. But my stomach aches with disgust. I know he's cheating on me, but I still accept his phone calls from Santa Rita.

90

I still go to school with sandbags under my eyes from walking from Chestnut in West Oakland to Emeryville with no money. I get there two periods too late and rack up more detentions that I will never go to and more disapproval from my teachers. I'm on Shep's shit list. I go to class on autopilot. On last dollar days, I walk the aisles of Safeway or Lucky's grocery store and eat food straight from the shelf. I open up bottles of soda and juices and sip while I walk. I stuff grapes in my mouth while white ladies shake their heads.

The coach of the football team has me in his scope. 'Big Blue' pulls alongside me in his big blue K-5 with lust in his eyes. All the high school girls have a crush on him. But he's been circling around me with a truck full of football players and his head out the window eyeballing my teenage figure. I'm spose to stay away from men like him. I ain't that into him anyway. But this day, this time, this moment, I have nowhere to turn. I let him pick me up one night and take me to a drive-in movie theater but after he tries to fuck me, I have him drive me back home to my dark house. I wait till he drives off and light my candle. Climbing those stairs is like what my life feels like; dark and empty. I'm in a hole and I can't see my way out. I walk into my mom's room where I sleep now and remove the coat that Tim's brother, John bought me and crawl under the covers. I hate my fuckin life.

Tim's brother John has come by one day to check on me and notices that I don't have a jacket. It's wintertime and it's cold. I've peeped a double goose jacket at Hilltop mall while I was out with Amina. John offers to take me to Hilltop and buy the $100 coat for me. Amina is supposed to ride with me, but she can't leave her house. I jump in his Benz 190 without her. He's smiling broad as the gate to hell. Before we hit the mall, he buys me a dime bag of weed. I fire it up. We roll to the mall and to my astonishment he buys the coat.

On the way home things get weird. He starts playing, *Cutie pie* by One-way on his car stereo and looking at me with his eyes glazed over in lust. I figure he's taking the long route but then the area starts to get more and more remote. When he slides down a side road by the airport and I can hear the tires grind to a halt on the gravel, my heart sinks. I'm staring straight ahead at the air freshener tree hanging from his rearview while he snorts some kind of narcotic. I never knew he was a bass-head.

He leans over and touches my breast. I swipe at his hands, "Stop." But I've seen those crazed eyes before. He tries again and when I hit his hand away the next time, he stops. He leans forward and reaches under his seat. When he pulls his hand up, he's holding a small handgun. I look at the door to see if it's unlocked. It isn't. He chuckles, "What you lookin at?" I stare at the gun in his hand with a thousand thoughts fighting in my head. *Jump out. Try to take it. Do whatever he says.* He rests the gun in his lap and puts his hand behind my seat. He looks like he's contemplating something. I sit quiet and motionless. I've decided to give him some if he tries. I feel his hands in my hair and cringe. He starts playing with my ear lobe and raps in my ear with his hot breath, "Just chill." I feel his mouth devouring my ear and I hear his tongue slithering in. I'm disgusted. Then he gets to the nitty gritty, "Take them pants off." *Come Again?* He starts rubbing on his groin like he thinks he's gonna get some head or something. "Come on." It ricochets off his lips in an authoritative tone. I feel like I'm five again under the sink at my mom's house. I'm still as a cat. I rethink my plan. I start thinking that his hands are occupied and that maybe I *can* take the gun. I visualize myself grabbing the gun in lightning speed and blowing his brains out. The voice in my head is screaming at me, just *grab it!* But my hands are heavy as bricks and don't move.

Then suddenly he stops. It's like he climbs back off the ledge. He leans back into his seat and starts the car. It's like his conscience has suddenly kicked back in. He pulls away from the dirt and back onto the road. I'm silent all the way home. He leaves me with an open invitation, "Call me if you need anything. But you know what time it is." I never call. I don't have enough for a coat, but I realize I really can't afford to be weak. I rock my coat and forget what it almost cost me.

Now I'm the cream of the crop at school. It seems that every boy likes me, and I wear all the other girls' envy like the crop tops and spaghetti straps with super short shorts I sport. I'm hurting. I wear my pain like my necklace. I dangle sexy from my neck, but no one knows the price I pay for its luster.

This one guy Johnny buys me lunch every day. He's a true captain-save-a-hoe and lollipop sucka sweet. I hit him for snacks and bus fare sometimes like he's my paperboy. I like Johnny but I can't relate to his boyish smile and innocent eyes. He's a church boy from a two-parent household. He's a preacher's kid with a genuine smile but someone should've told him that chivalry been dead. Why even pretend that he can do anything for me other than buy my lunch? I'm into a guy who drives a Corvette and likes getting high and sliding in between my 17-year-old thighs. Johnny needs a good girl. I ingest Tupac. I smoke cest.

I charge in front of Johnny in the lunch line, smacking my juicy fruit lips and he's quick to pay for my food. Now I'm sitting cross-legged on a bench stuffing my mouth with chili cheese fries bought with his chore money and he's trying to tell me he likes me for the ten thousandth time. Boy talk is cheap. I hear him but I act like I don't. I shoot down his compliments faster than they can come. He has everyone wondering what so damn good about me. The hell if I know. Maybe when he tells them he can tell me too.

Now he's all in my personal space breathing all down my damn neck with childish eyes. He smiles at me shyly looking in my eyes like he's searching for heaven, "You want to go the prom with me?"

My eyes cut him like scissors, "Hell nawl."

I laugh just as hard as his friends. I get up and walk off annoyed. I ain't thinkin about the damn prom boy. I don't even have any food at home. *Fuck a prom*. I got bigger fish to fry. I leave his ego in ruins. I don't need no glass slipper or yellow brick road. I need cash. He's like a little kid to me sulking and looking all sad. *Toobadfuckyasorryforyou*. I ain't the chick he thinks I am. I steal a glance back at him. There's a part of me that wishes I could be her.

19: The Cost of Living

Delana's pregnant. I find out two weeks before the baby comes. She pull's me to the side by the locker and confirms what everyone suspected, "I'm pregnant."
I'm shocked, "By who?" ...*then comes a baby in a baby carriage...*

She looks around to make sure we're alone and tells me a dude in West Oakland who she met on the bus raped her one day when she went to visit him. I'm furious, "Why didn't you tell me?" I'd been defending her and damn near fighting people spreading rumors about her. I damn near come to blows with people over these rumors. I look at her over-sized belly and I want to slap myself for not knowing. She hasn't told anyone but me and she's 9 months and about to burst. I question her about the guy. I don't know if I believe her. I do, however, understand that she can't tell her mom. Her little sister Queen has already dropped out and ran away from home. We hear rumors about her being ran through in East Oakland. Delana has three brothers in prison with lengthy sentences. She doesn't want to burden her mom any more than she already is. I feel her. The funny thing is when she does tell her, her mom yells at me like I'm a bad influence, "You tramp, you the reason Delana is pregnant. She shouldn't have been hanging with you." Everyone knows my mom isn't around much and I do whatever I want to do. *But I'm not the one pregnant, though.*

I'm walking with Amina, whose flipping thru the yearbook reading me the senior polls. They've been tallied and everyone is excited. She has been voted "Best Dressed" and I can see why. She gasps, "Girl guess who got Most Attractive?" I shrug, thinking it's probably Raquel or somebody really cute. She's jumping up and down now, "You!!!" I barely hear her. I'm frozen still. Why? Because I see my name on the Graduation list. *What the?* I'm dumbfounded. I have 10,000 butterflies in my belly. Shep all but

94

guaranteed me that I had so many detentions and Saturday schools racked up that it'd be impossible to make them up. Plus, my teachers have been pencil whipping me with all kinds of behavior documents. I even started school a few days later than the other students this year because I had been suspended on the last day of school for fighting the previous year. So, my name on that list seems like a huge mistake. Amina is whispering behind me, "Damn you in there, huh?" I'm confused. "I guess so."

I'm secretly excited. I stay under the radar while everyone prepares for graduation day buying senior photos and class rings. I don't have any money, but Amina steals me a cap and gown. I thought Shep would realize his mistake and remove me from the list, but he doesn't. I know I don't have the credits. I meet with Mr. Buckley, the Science teacher whose class I bombed with the balloons that day. He shakes his head when he sees me coming. I'm all eyes and teeth but his expression isn't friendly. I know I haven't been to his class much this semester. He's stern faced when I ask if there is anything, I can do to make up the credits. He shakes his head, "Jennifer you have really dug yourself into a hole, haven't you?" I cock my neck back. He checks the roster and breathes a heavy sigh, "You missed two reports and several assignments." I look over at all the empty boxes by my name, "I can do them." He sounds doubtful, "I need them by the end of the week." I go to Ms. McKinney's algebra class. I hate math. The only facts I can add up are being black, female in a single parent home. Negatives never equaled a positive in my world plus I barely know my times tables. I sing her a long woe is me song.

I visit Mr. Campbell, the teacher I walked out on. I threw up the finger to him and Drivers Education when he asked me to buy some maps because it was easier than explaining not having the money for a $3 map. When I ask to meet with him, he laughs, "I knew you'd be back."

My teachers know I'm a good writer. They are still praising my poem. I offer to make up all my work by way of essays. I write six reports for my teachers in place of missed assignments. Mr.

Campbell gives me an assignment called the Cost of Living. In the paper I have to give a report on what it will cost for me to die. I have to tally up funeral expenses, ambulance and hospital costs as well as burial fees. At the end of the paper, I conclude that I really can't afford to die, logically speaking. I turn it in to him and he gives me full credit. I wing a math exam on a hope and a prayer.

I'm running down San Pablo Ave with my graduation forms getting wet from rain. I cover my face with my elbow, leaning on the payphone and call Tia to share the news. "Bitch I made it!" I'm so excited. Tia's mom has gotten clean, remarried and moved Tia and her little sister out of the hood and into El Sobrante Hills so I barely see her. They moved up like the Jefferson's. I'm giddy when I share with her the big news of the day. But she doesn't respond. I'm like, 'Hello? Did you hear me?" Tia's voice is flat and void of emotion, "My mom died."

My mind spirals, "What?"

Tia explains it to me like she's talking about the weather, but the impact is like point blank range, "She died last night at the hospital. She had AIDS."

Damn, I knew she was sick but *AIDS*? Turns out Tia's mother had contracted AIDS during her years of prostitution and drug use, and it has caught up to her with a vengeance. I flash back to Tia's mom beating her in the kitchen with an aluminum foil holder and chasing us down the stairs yelling that we are selling our bodies to men. I knew she was haunted by demons of her past. I knew she was an addict, but she had just gotten cleaned up. I just never imagined this. They've all been tested now. Her baby sister, Necia, also has the disease. I guess it ain't no rainbows without no rain. Tia buries her mother, Delana has her baby and me and Amina walk the stage at our High School Graduation.

19 hundred and 94. Maceo and Yusef are my sole supporters in the gymnasium when I get my diploma. Yusef 's rockin his black medallion with red, black and green on it. Maceo

has two kids now and one on the way. He quituated in junior high but he's jumping up and down yelling, "My muthafuckin patna!"

When he hands me my diploma, Shep-dog gives me a hug and says, "I'm glad to see you on the stage, Jennifer." I look doubtful when he says, "You should use your writing talent. You're an artist. You have enough imagination to make the pain in this world art."

When I'm posing with my girls on the yard taking pictures, I see my mom and Tim. At first, I'm confused. I haven't seen her in months. She's smiling and hugging me and shit saying, 'I'm so glad we finally made it." *Huh?* Does she realize I'm living in the dark in an empty house? Does she realize I raided her scraps of left behind clothes to put together this outfit just to look decent today? Does she realize I don't even have electricity to curl my hair, so I went to a shop and begged them to hook me up for my big day? Does she even know that I have everything I own in garbage bags in Amina's new jeep cause I ain't going back to West Oakland? I'm frozen stiff while she poses for Tim's disposable camera shots. Then he takes me off guard and hands my mom the camera and slides his arms around my slender waist. It's weird. He's holding me in a bear hug with his face to my cheek. My mom is all smiles behind the lens. In the picture I have a look of utter confusion.

20: So Many Tears

It's 1995 and California is a hot bed of political activism following the King riots and the OJ Simpson Trial. 15-year-old Latasha Harlins was shot and killed by a Korean store owner; a black girl's life worth less than a bottle of orange juice it seems. I guess you can say I don't know my place. I've been living from pillar to post dragging my clothes with me. Sometimes I beg people to allow Tia to stay too. Tia has been on her own since her mom passed from AIDS and her mother's husband ran off with all the money. She's like a nymphomaniac now though. I think she's slowly becoming her mom circa 1980. If she doesn't stay with me there's always some guy's bed, she can lay in. But the stay often ends at the tail end of a nut in the wee hours of the night and she's dragging herself to where I am anyway. I've gotten fired from Ross for stealing so I have no income and nowhere to stay. Me and Tia walk all the way to the West Oakland McDonald's, but they won't hire us. We fill out applications everywhere we can but by the end of the day we don't find work and she's up under another dude's wet balls and I'm on the couch fighting off his friend.

I apply for General Assistance and get $150.00 every two weeks that I try to save to afford to get me a place.
I beg my mother's friend to let me stay at her house in exchange for babysitting. It all falls down. Two months in, she robs me of the $300 I saved from GA. One day I open the closet and my stash is gone. No one knows shit about it. I kick rocks. I got $30 in my pocket. I'm unable to apply for food stamps because my mother and Tim still get have me on their case as a dependent. I meet a guy on the train, and I spend the night at a motel with him. He steals my $30 while I'm sleeping. When I wake up, I find my raided purse on the floor of the motel. I scratch up 75 cent and hit the slab walking. My last resort is riding the bus to Alameda where Krystal now stays. When I knock on her door, she opens it with a worried look on her face. "Where you been?"

98

I tell her I'm broke and ain't got nowhere to stay-again. She lets me sleep in her garage. The skeletal remains of who her mom used to be is sitting on the couch clutching a juice box. Her mom stares past me when I walk in. She's slowly learning to walk and talk again but it's weighing on Krystal. Krystal is on Section 8 and has a nice two-bedroom house and she's caring for her 8-year-old brother like she's his mom. Christmastime rolls around and I feel even more worthless watching them decorate for the holidays. It's like the ghost of my poor Christmas past comes to haunt me whenever the holidays come around. Even when I lived with my mom, I didn't get gifts but for some reason watching someone else celebrate eats away at my joy. I slip casual sex into the garage every now and then but I still feel lonely.

I told Krystal I'd find a way to get her some money so I can pitch in. I'm walking back to Krystal's house with my skintight blue dress on exhausted from filling out applications. I see a red truck hit the corner with Biggie Smalls playing loud from the speaker system,

I love it when they call me big poppa...

My heart leaps when the window rolls down and I see Suinjata's 20-watt smile, "What's up Tenda Roni!" I'm jumping up and down like a little girl now. He pulls over and I jump in onto the crack vinyl seat, "N—I—g—gg—a, how did you find me?" He's all pearly whites, "I asked Delana, she told me you were at Krystal's." I run down my raggedy ass circumstance and he waves his hands, "Fuck that. Go get your shit. I'm getting an apartment out this way by the beach." The cinnamon-tobacco scent of his JOOP cologne is comforting. I missed him.

I can't even believe it myself when he pulls up at Buena Vista apartments and puts the whole $1500 deposit down. He pays first and last month's rent in hundreds like a boss. I peep Suinjata's gear. He's preppy now, all clean-cut like a college boy. His haircut's fresh. His white Nike's glistening. A gold chain is dangling from his neck like a trophy. He tells me Delana and them are all on his jock now. He's been working as a disc jockey at the University of California. He's been throwing a lot of parties with big name celebs like Ice Cube and Charli Baltimore. I laugh with him but I'm thinking, *Damn Sin you got it going on.* Then a small Honda Accord swoops into the parking space beside him. A platinum blond light-skinned chick beautiful as Halle Berry steps out. He introduces me to his girlfriend, Maya. College life has been good to my friend.

The first night me and Sin sleep on the floor and share a blanket singing a duet of poverty. We ain't got shit but his crates of records and DJ equipment. As soon as we unlocked the door, we'd run through the house and screamed like we were George and Weezy and this is our deluxe apartment. He insists I get the big room. I pretend to argue but happily accept. He ain't used to no space anyway he says, "I ain't used to shit." He's just kindhearted like that. He buys me and Maya diamond Christmas gifts from Zales and we giggle like little girls.

The next Day Yusef and Krystal roll up in a big ass U-Haul yelling from the truck like they stole something. They came to drop off old furniture that they aren't using. Yusef's getting married! He doesn't need his old stuff. He jumps out the truck popping the collar of a crispy UPS outfit, "Ya boy got a real job!" I grab the Futon. Sin grabs a mattress. I fall asleep to the soundtrack of Sin and his girlfriend having a jam session on the mattress and everywhere else in the house with The Notorious BIG's record spinning on his turntable,

> To all the ladies in the place with style and grace
> Allow me to lace these lyrical douches in your bushes
> Who rock grooves and make moves with all the mamis?

We're broke as hell, but Sin is music in an empty space- he feels the room with his vibe. He throws parties to pay the rent and our apartment is always bumper to bumper with rap dudes and homegirls partying till the break of dawn. Soon we have strobe lights bouncing off our black leather couches and sparkling off the black and brass tables. We hang a Scarface poster in the dining room next to a fold-up card table and toss an ash tray in the center. He isn't asking anything from me until I find a job. I got cut-offs riding up showing off my cocoa to the beat of TLC's "Creep" *Oooh ahhh, oooh ahhhhh*

Sin knows I'm a go-getter and I will come up with the money come hell or high negroes. Meanwhile I'm meeting guys and handing out sex like it's my demo. I meet a guy named Leo at his party, boom he's at the crib on the futon and we doing it doggy style. We fuck to DJ Quick. But I'm in control. I don't even give a shit if he calls me tomorrow. That's how it goes down in Buena Vista apartment 52. Sin puts a cup to the door and listens to me stroke niggas egos.

Saturday night hip hop beats off Sin's 1000-watt speakers and turntables. Sin's sipping vodka with his shirt off, eyes radiating like a sky full of stars. Maya is pouring water on her chest like it's a wet t-shirt contest. She's dancing cum drunk off Sin. There's a symphony of voices laughing, talking and rapping. It's a moment of living. I sit on my windowsill and look out at a bunch of young guys on a sofa sitting in the middle of our apartment complex watching, a fresh out of jail, Mike Tyson beat the brakes off Peter McNeeley on a big screen that someone dragged into the yard. Tyson's fist burst like lightening into McNeely and the crowd erupts, "Get that white boy!" Tyson is the angry black man's champion; a warrior for the under-dog. I watch Sin grabbing his soaking wet lady by her waist and try to talk sexy in his nasally voice. She's kissing his bronze chest. He pushes her down on my Futon. I watch their session for a minute then turn back to the window. The music doesn't drown out the sounds of their lovemaking.

Grand Auto hires me. I work honestly for a few months but then my old thieving ways get the best of me. I start small on the register and work my way up to big deposit licks. By the time I get Suinjata involved, it's moved into grand theft arena. I'm slipping credit cards to his girlfriend and they are going insane in the stores while I'm on the clock. This bitch is rocking new Jordan's and Doonie and Burke purses. He's lacing her down with jewelry and Victoria Secrets. It makes me furious. Now we're arguing all the time. We doin all this hustling but he's letting her pimp us both.

I get all in his face, "Stop re-using the cards"

He's red, "Stop trippin."

"Stop being a mark! Stop buying this bitch all these shoes like some weak ass nigga."

He starts freestyle rapping on the microphone entertaining his friends and calls me a bitch in his rhyme. They laugh.

I slap his ass.

All the air sucks out of the room.

Sin stares at me long.

He picks me up and slams me through my bedroom door and bodies me into my Futon. His homeboys come to the door while he has me straddled and pinned by my arms.

I'm trying to kick myself free.

They shake their head, "Aye yo we out of here. Ya'll trippin."

It's the beginning of the end. He is letting the credit cards turn him into a mad man. Now he's pressuring me to hit more licks, "If you bring in some more Platinum cards instead of these wack ass Visa's, we good." It turns out this is more successful than his parties. I hustle harder.

I put my scheme into high gear. A white lady comes in and lays her purse down. I swoop her card. An old man is distracted while paying for his order, I sneak his card. I have my eye on the prize. Maya comes in and I slide it to her and place my order like it's a drive-thru, "A TV/VCR combo." Sin's outside with the truck running. He's turning into a beast with the credit cards, shopping every day. I try to warn him to slow down but he doesn't. Then the clock stops. The police catch him filling his tank up with gas on a stolen Visa with a truck full of stolen merchandise. He gets arrested and I get robbed for most of our stolen goods. Then I get caught. Now I need money bad. I can't keep up me and Sin's rent on the $5/hr wage I earn.

I climb the stairs to the admins office of my job and beg my supervisor for more money. He's a white guy with a permanent frown on his face. He doesn't even look at me when he says, "It's not in the budget.
I smirk, "Yeah ok." *Fuck a budget.*
I decide to hit a massive lick at my job. A customer lays a shitload of cash on the counter in front of me and my mind reels to unpaid bills, bus fair, food, and bullshit. I know I should stick to cards, but this big wad of cash is calling my name. I've been watching the cash deposits and I come up with a scheme that would make Robin Hood blush. I've watched the manager log-in. I know his passwords. I go in and fandangle the drop amounts. I think I pull off the heist of the century. Later that night the cops are knocking at my door. Word is already in the street and the ghetto grapevine brings me the juice before the cops can make it around the hood. They visited some of my old haunts looking for me and now the word is out. They went to Krystal's house and visited Delana's mom's house. I know I'm in deep shit, but I just don't know how much or what for.
****

I lay in jail thinking, damn this is the road my life has taken. I'm ashamed of myself. I'm in a holding cell for 11 hours before I see the judge. Afterwards I'm in the felony tank watching women get high on dope they smuggled in inside their coochies and trying to sleep under the backdrop of girls making love to girls. I can't eat the bland food they serve us. My stomach is cramping. I try to call my mom. She wants to send me a package like I'm in the pen. I tell her, "Mom I'm in the County you can't send that here." I

103

reach out to Sin's homeboys. No answer. Jaybird has someone pay the bail for me and I'm back on the street the next day waiting on a sentencing court date. He tells me to deny everything. I have no intention on telling the truth.

The day I get out I catch the bus home and walk up to see a red eviction notice blowing against my door. Its's a friendly notice to vacate directly from the Sherriff's office. I open the door to white walls and records all over the floor. We been robbed--again. Back to zero.

21: G.H.E.T.T.O.U.T. Jbird gets out and swoops

me up in his cocaine white beamer smiling his Ice-Cube-it's-a-good -day smile. He has a house now in the Oakland hills. I snuggle next to him and dream about moving in and being a housewife. He has a Jacuzzi and Jet skis. It's like some other level type of stuff. I been down like 4 flats writing him and taking his calls, but I fail to mention that after the things that happened with Suinjata and the arrest that I been evicted out of the apartment.

Before I can sit comfortably in his arms, he catches a federal King Pen charge. It won't be any getting out for a while. He calls me from the pen in a panic because he's afraid he's going to die.
I laugh out, "Yeah ok. You been to jail before dude."
His voice is different, "Yeah but this time I'm fucked."
I think I got game, "You good, it won't be much time."
"I'ma tell em I'm on dope. I'm a user. I need help." Breathing heavy.
I laugh again, "That ain't gonna work. Everybody says that shit"
"I got Heroine in my system. If I don't get some, I'm gonna die tonite." It hits me like a cold shock. *Huh?*
He's vomiting and becoming incoherent. I hang up.
I don't even mention that I'm six weeks pregnant.
not 'cuz I'm dirty
not 'cuz I'm clean
just 'cuz I kissed a boy behind a magazine

I'm burned out. With nowhere else to go I take the only open doors I see- my mom and Tim. To my surprise Tim is happy to see me. When I walk in the door, he looks me up and down and helps me with my bags. I'm dumb founded. My stomach isn't really showing yet. My mom and him have moved to School Street into a depressed one bedroom flat beside a liquor store ran by some Arab guys who sell liquor on the front end and guns under the table. My mom and Tim tell me I can catch the couch. They have gotten married. My mom has found some small penny- any job and she leave every day at 8am to catch the bus downtown. Tim is still doing what he does best-nothing. As soon as she leaves Tim is coming into the living room making small talk. I look at him suspiciously wondering what's with this new niceness. Today he's made me some eggs. I can't eat them. I'm sick and everything smells horrible. He sits in the armchair and prods me, "You got to eat something." I try to swallow down a few bites of slimy eggs and go back to sleep.

He returns later and starts up the chatter again. I roll over to find him looking at me hard through his glasses. I don't know what to make of this new Tim.

The next day when my mom leaves, he's back in there like clockwork trying to talk with me about random things. He's trying to appear to be just shooting the breeze and then he drops a hint like a tiny morsel to see if I'm hungry enough to bite it, "So that boy in that Vette got you pregnant?" I shake my head, yes. He's nodding like he's thinking then he say's "I bet yawl had sex all the time, huh?" I turn to face him. I'm looking like, what kind of question is that? But he has a dreamy look in his eyes like he's imagining it. I try to turn back over but he won't let it go, "I bet he loves that little young pussy." My eyes bulge. Did I just hear this negro right?

It's the same every day. When my mom leaves, he's on me like flies on shit. He's following me around the house dropping hints, like the devil whispering in my ear. He keeps me in his scope all the time. He wants to buy me weed but I don't smoke now that I'm pregnant. He's talking to me about Vegas and how much money young girls like me can make on the strip out there. He say's I'm pretty so I'll make a killing. He says I'm beautiful enough to appeal to white men. He asks me do I want to go with him to Vegas. He starts telling me sick details about him and my mom's sex life or lack thereof, "You know she is timid in the bed. But I bet you're feisty. You know what to do." He follows me to the kitchen and takes aim, "You know you want to give me some."

I share it with Amina. She's pregnant now too as a result of a Ménage trois gone wrong and now has her own problems. I don't know what else to do. I really need to stay here. I'm pregnant and I don't have nowhere else to go. Amina cautions me, "Don't say shit cause he's gonna lie." But it starts getting so out of hand. He's eyeballing me running his tongue over his lip, "They say pregnant pussy is the best. I know it's wet." He's looking at my breast because they are getting big and plump with my pregnancy. All this time I thought Tim hated me and now he's around here acting like I'm God's gift to men. He's telling me every freaky thing he wants to do to me. I try to ignore him as much as I can but it's getting ridiculous. I'm not combative because I feel like I need him and my mom. I been out on the streets since 1994. It's been brutal. But still, I can't take Tim's constant badgering me for sex. So, I decide to tell my mom.

I lay it all out to her with all cards facing up. She's sipping her Coffee quietly and listening to me intently. Once I start telling her it's like a dam breaks and I can't stop talking. I tell her every foul thing he ever said to me. I tell her how he is trying to get me to move into another apartment with him, just me and him. My mother is looking stunned and asking me strange questions like, "What are you wearing when I go to work?" I'm confused, "Same thing I always wear." She shakes her head, "Nise I told you to stop walking around the house with no bra on." *Huh?* I try to remember if I have on bras or not. Her face is drawn in like she's thinking. Her eyes are narrow, and her lips are tight. It's silent for a long time and she finally says, "I'll talk to him."
I walk into the kitchen and run dish water. The house is awkwardly silent. I'm half-way through washing the dishes when I turn around and I'm shocked to see my mother still sitting in the same exact spot on the couch staring at me. It's uncomfortable because she isn't looking at me in my eyes but instead her eyes

are roaming up and down my body like she's sizing me up. She hasn't realized that I'm looking at her. When she sees me, she smirks and quietly gets up from the couch and walks off. I don't know what to think. I keep washing dishes and try to stay out of the way. I'm convinced she hates me.

I wait all day for the axe to fall but nothing happens. It isn't until the next day when I come home that I see my dirty laundry spilled out on the living room floor. I look from her to Tim's smirking face. She's standing there with her arms folded while Tim kneels down and searches through my clothes. My soiled panties and bras are strewn about. Humiliated, I shriek, "What are ya'll doing?" My mom snaps, "Tim said you've been wearing my panties." I look from her to him. Clearly there aren't any of her panties in my dirty clothes hamper. Then she spits out the real information she wants to give me, "Tim said he hasn't tried anything with you." I step back like she hit me across the face, "He's lying." Tim throws his hands up like this conversation is beneath him and walks off. I yell at his back, "You're a fuckin liar." I know what's happening. My mom is looking at the floor. I stare at her, but she can't look at me when she says, "You have to leave." She's just a constant reminder of what I don't want to be. I watch her sit on the couch and it's a funeral procession of tears as usual.

I don't cry as I gather my dirty clothes and hit the block walking into the cold arms of the night. My eyes are stones. I ain't got nowhere to go, again.

22: 3:16.

I haven't really been to church too much. When I was little the church van would pull up and carry me and my brothers to Sunday school while my mother dozed. I remember carrying a little passage in my pocket from the verse 3:16 and studying it. My Sunday school teacher had given us all a passage and 3:16 was my verse. I owned it. I would walk and repeat it to myself over and over. I was so happy when I had it memorized. *For God so loved the world, he sent his only begotten Son for those who believe in him should not perish but have ever-lasting life.*
Perish (verb)
1.
to die or be destroyed through violence, privation, etc.:

2.
to suffer destruction or ruin:

I walk the streets with no aim. I'm defeated. My spirit is empty. I don't even care anymore. I don't even think about where I'm going to sleep. I just walk against the wind in a stupor with my dirty belongings in a garbage bag. I'm tired of climbing hills of despair only to find another mountain in front of me. I feel like I've worn out all the welcome mats. I firmly believe it is God that has Toni walking the streets that same day at that same time. Toni: Puerto Rican chick with bug eyes. I know I know her from somewhere. It hits me: *Planned Parenthood.* Sitting in the lobby waiting on test results.
Pregnancy test: positive
Father: Married man
Live births: 2
Plan: abortion
I told her I might do the same. According to the nurse that's the only option a girl in my circumstances has. Toni had cautioned me in a lifeless voice, "Don't do it unless you can live with it." I walked

out with abortion pamphlets in my hand but a child on my conscience.

Today that same chick is getting off at the bus stop near School Street and she recognizes me, "What up girlie?" I wave mechanically but I can't even fake a smile. I don't know if she sees hope sinking in my eyes, but she throws a life raft, "Check this out. I need someone to take this weave out my head. Can you come through?"
I follow her home just grateful to have a detour from nowhere. I untangle my life like the 19inch 1b yaky I'm pulling from her corn rolls. She unravels hers: she's just as broke, she ain't got no food but she has a couch I can sleep on it. She takes my conversation for payment. Her kids are bad, and they run around recklessly but if I can help her pack and get them together, I can stay as long as I need to. The girl makes wonders from the food we drag home from the free food pantry at the neighborhood church. While I'm loading food into a cardboard box, I notice a scripture written in red on the walls of the church, John 3:16. I smile inside.

Later, my mouth melts into the nutmeg beans Toni makes. I listen to her in the morning as she prays. She's in her room begging the Lord to help her. It's like she's talking to God for me in the cloudiness of my doubt, "Lord please guide me. Give me direction. I feel like I'm all by myself Lord." I recognize the pain in her voice. I'm familiar with gripping loneliness and despair. She's putting her kids on the Greyhound the next day going to Texas, but she tells me that I can get on welfare like her, "You qualify. You need to go get some food stamps and a check cause you pregnant." She packs the remainder of the beans into sandwich bags for their two-day bus ride to Texas and schools me on 'the system.' She only has a few dollars left but she gives me bus fare and a couple dollars to hold me over. I want to get on the bus with her. I wave by.
When I leave Toni's, I go to the welfare office. The sad metal doors of the aide office open wide as the gates of hell. As

soon as I walk into the ocean of people I get discouraged. It's a black tragedy in four parts: Medicaid, food stamps, childcare and General assistance. There's a maze of lines and numbers zigzagging through-out the old building. Signs scream, *"NO pen, NO paper so don't even ask!* It's a hell for the fallen. The bottom of the food chain. There's dog-tired single moms in dime-store casual clothes. Women reduced to babymamas, big mamas, and welfare queens. They are scattered about like bits and pieces of shattered homes. There's wailing BeBe's kids, shadows of homeless men, and all other broken spirits roaming the bottomless pit of government assistance. I'm miss-anony-miss. Just another welfare recipient.

A rail thin dope fiend is at the window cursing at the case worker behind the bullet proof glass, "Hoe I been in line all day. I ain't gone back" I join the wealth of poor people below the poverty line that has the letter "A "taped to a metal pole. A homeless lady standing near me stinking with the smell of defeat, smiles at me, "You a pretty lil ole girl. You got a dollar I can have?" *Bitch I'm homeless too.* By the time I fill out the 20-page questionnaire I'm exhausted. *Do you have a car? No. Do you have any cash on hand? No. Do you own any property?* ~~Hell~~ No. Emotionally broke. I haven't eaten. I go to a convenience store to buy something to get me through the day. I'm standing in the line with some Funyuns and a pack of Big Red gum. I'm nauseous. I shift from foot to foot waiting, but I start to feel woozy. As I wait for the long-winded person in front of me to pay for their items my body starts tingling. I feel strange. The Arab guy at the counter is yelling to me to pay but it sounds like I'm in a faraway tunnel and his voice is droning in and out. He's fading away. I try to take a step toward the counter, but I feel like I'm walking down invisible stairs. I never feel myself crumble. I just wake up and realize that it's my arm that I'm looking at on the floor. I black out again. I fade back into people running around and trying to force water in my mouth. I listen to them ramble for a minute. Then, I collect myself slowly from the floor, pulling down my dress and stand up on wobbly legs. I sip more water from a styro-foam cup someone hands me. The Arab cashier shakes his head at me like I'm just another drug head. A girl asks him to call an ambulance, but I wave her off. She looks at me like I'm crazy. I'm not crazy, I'm broke. I can't afford an ambulance.

I'm back at the welfare office in a big Starter jacket and dingy jeans. The welfare office is still full of lines of people all needing something. I wait hours in the cold chairs for my number to be called. With each hour my hope is decomposing even more. The Case Worker, a middle-aged heavy-set black woman with a lop-sided wig is taking my information without really looking at me. I'm just a number in a chair. How much money do I have on me? *A buck and a prayer.* I tell her I'm six months pregnant.

She asks me my address. I tell her I don't have one. She asks me my age.

I say, "19."

She stops typing and finally looks me over, taking in my 115lb body. She asks with a frown, "Where you staying?"

I shake my head. I can't say anything. I'm ashamed. I see something bizarre in her eyes. She excuses herself for a moment. I sit there looking at the posters on the walls of the babies and their mothers. I think about my baby. I trace my fingers on my small tummy and he plays me a beat back. I'm happy I still feel movement cause I know he's still alive. I try to wrap my brain around the fact that I am going to be someone's mother. I just hope his father can become a daddy in 9 months, 40 weeks and 280 days when I become a mama. When the lady returns, she has a wad of cash in her hand. I almost bust out crying when she lays forty dollars in the plexi glass window.

She taps the glass with her long artificial nail and demands, "You get off these streets."

My shoulders slump and the weight of it all now seems too heavy. My vision gets cloudy. I can't hold back the rain.

She nods her head, "I know baby." Now tears are flaming down my cheek. She gets up again and brings me a slip of paper, "These are shelters. Call the numbers on this list. Until you find one you need to go to a motel. If you bring me the motel receipt each day, I'll give you more money." I grab the money and paper like hope. I want to kiss her. I want her to take me home. I want to be her daughter.

I ride the bus looking out the dirty window for a motel that I can stay in for under 40 bucks. An Asian boy leans across the back of the seat and propositions me, "You wanna make some money?" He has an eager-eyed Asian woman with him. I don't know what they have planned, and I don't care. I brush past them. I just saw a small run-down spot in East Oakland. It's a comfortable sleep under the backdrop of whores and dope fiends. I don't eat. The cold night is nothing to me. I'm accustomed to being without food. I lay in the dark and look at the raggedy yellow paged bible on the nightstand and feel like I'm not alone. I think about my baby and visualize what it will look like.

In the morning I'm back at the window and true to her word, The Case manager slides more money to me. "Good! Now here's two nights worth." I grab the money ready to run. Then she does something remarkable, she steps away from the window, opens the big wooden door and reaches out to me. I damn near fall into her big hug. I smell flowery perfume in her breast. She rubs my hair back into place. Her eyes are a refuge in this storm. Still, embracing a woman seems strange to me. My mother is not affectionate. But this woman is tender and warm. I usually feel awkward around women, but her smile is easy.

She whispers to me, "I found you a shelter." She guides me by my hand and sits me down in the metal chairs and tells me about CASA Vincentia. It's a shelter for young pregnant homeless girls. She says she's talked to them and they want to see me. Her voice is therapeutic, "They have to interview you to see if you fit in their program." She warns me like she knows I'm a wild child, "You have to be ready to be structured." I nod and try to look honest. I hope I fit so bad. I spend the next night tossing and turning thinking about the shelter. What will it be like? I picture a line of homeless drunks and smelly old men. I think I'll probably have to fight for respect. I'm ready I was born into ruckus and never had no dignity I didn't win with my fist. That night I dream about my baby and imagine myself getting my license and driving him in a convertible along the Oakland shoreline. I have stupid visions of going to ball games with him. I know it's a boy, I can feel it.

23: CASA.

I don't know where broken hearts go but I need a place to call home. I'm clicking my boots against the pavement saying to myself, *There's no place like home.* I catch the bus through despair and hike up the steep hills of heartache to 62nd Ave in East Oakland. The shelter at 3201 is housed in the former convent of St. Cyril Parish and is owned by the Roman Catholic Diocese of Oakland. It sits smack dab in the middle of one of East Oakland's crack alley's and on this rock, they built this church. Guys scream at me from across the street, but I ignore them, I feel like I'm on a mission.

I approach the door and notice the big wooden cross on it and an inscription that reads, "There is no greater gift than the gift of giving." I feel like God is reaching out to me, like even through the fighting, cussing and sexing, he heard my feeble prayer. I ring the doorbell and wait, resting my bag on my boot. Then a white nun opens the door with the broadest smile I ever seen in my life, "You must be Jennifer," Damn *white people be too happy.* She smiles with her eyes. She speaks simple and modest. I tense as she wraps her arms along my shoulder. I stand there awkwardly as she informs me, "My name is Elaine." I try hard to smile. I want her to like me. Elaine is a frail old white lady with wrinkle lines all over her elfish face. She's dressed in full traditional nun's black fabric dress and simple black shoes like she stepped right out a time warp. I'm standing in the hall in a sweater and leggings with scratches on my neck from fighting and tired looking eyes. I shift when I say "yes," showing my discomfort. But Elaine wisps me into a big living room like a fairy god mother dragging me through Oz.

The place is serene and bright like something out of a Home and Garden book. There's plush colorful pillows everywhere. It's a house full of baby mamas of all nationalities and they nod at me as I pass them. She announces, "Everyone this is Jennifer." She say's my name in proper English. There's girls walking from the spacious kitchen waving. There's girls on the veranda. Elaine walks me down a long hallway that's as long as a dormitory and has rooms up and down each side. There's a winding staircase that leads to the second floor. She points up there, "We have rooms upstairs also." The bathrooms are dorm style as well with individual stalls and showers all over one big area. She tells me, "Everyone contributes their food stamps and Wic and we prepare our meals together as a family." *Family?* I see big industrial sized appliances in the kitchen, "We're like one big family. A white girl is folding clothes in the laundry. We all have chores and responsibilities. Oh, and there's a curfew." Each girl has her own beautifully decorated room whose furniture and décor has been donated by various people and organizations.

At the end of the big hall upstairs she pushes open a door into a tangerine painted room. Inside there's a big-boned black girl about my age whose belly is standing out in front of her. I waddle in. Elaine says, "This is Jennifer. Jennifer this is Peaches." She nods. I nod. Her eyes are telling me a story I know way too well.

I sit down in a wooden chair in Elaine's study. Her work area is very practical. There is just a basic desk and wooden chairs. On the wall is a picture of the Blessed Virgin Mary with the halo of light above her head. There is a plaque with their motto, "Welfare is a stepping-stone, not a resting place... and that abstinence plus education equals independence and success."
Elaine smiles warmly at me, "How are you feeling today?"
I shrug, "shitty."
I look at her suspiciously when she writes something down on the pad she has.
"Why do you think you will be a good fit in our program?"
I'm puzzled, "I was told to come here." I'm combative. My fight or flight response kicks in and I'm ready to blow this joint. This fake ass nun and her lily-white house isn't for me. I can't relate.

"Sure. I understand. What do you hope to gain from CASA Vincentia?"

The question baffles me. My mind is tangled with thoughts. I don't know what she wants from me. I just tell her the truth, "I need a place to stay." I'm annoyed that she's writing, "What you writing?"

She puts her pencil down and talks softly like I'm a child, "Do you want to be here?"

My heart say's *hell yeah* but my face is a mask of toughness. I shrug my shoulders. I don't think this white lady can understand this ghetto shit.

I think about the smiling girls in the other room. I won't fit in. Elaine reels me back to our conversation, "Jennifer," I hate that she keeps calling my name, "If you want to be here you are going to have to unpack your things. First, we don't allow toxic language in CASA. There's no such thing as helplessness. You can and you must. There is no in between. There is no drug use here. There is no sex."

My eyes lift, *huh?*

She goes on, "Everyone here works to earn their keep. You contribute everything you have to the house. You cook, clean and you will sew everything you need for your baby." *Sew...bitch.*

She isn't done, "You will learn the importance of breastfeeding and nutritional eating. We believe in self-preservation. Above all else you will learn to be self-sufficient."

When she finishes, I am just starring at her lock jawed like she's speaking a foreign language. I'm ready to leave. I didn't care. Now, I give a shit-less. I don't know what she's waiting for. I think I have failed, and I am ready to go. Running is my norm.

She exhales and stands up, "We'd love to have you."

I inhale the words like breath.

PEACHES

I always loved the sweet smell of fresh rain and the way it hits the ground like a steady beat. It reminds me of music. It's October 1995. I'm 3 months pregnant. I look around my room at this pregnancy shelter and think to myself, *Damn. I've gone from Foster home to Homeless shelter. The next step is homeless bitch*. I used to watch the rain at my foster home, thinking some handsome guy who got his whole life together is gonna come swoop me up and let me share his world like the prince in the romance novels I read. Shit, who am I kidding? This shit only happens to white women. I'm far from a white girl. I ain't never even seen no yellow brick road and it damn sure ain't coming out of West Oakland.

Creak, creak, creak is the sound the rocking chair makes. I was on a good path before I got pregnant. Now I'm in this shelter without a pot to piss in or a window to throw it out of, as my granny would say before she died. She was my only relative. My mother is a Heroin addict and my father, "ran into some bullshit," as he put it. This is some serious bullshit. How the hell did my life turn out like this? Young, black, broke, homeless, pregnant and soon to be one thing I never wanted to be, JB's baby mama.

I'm 21 years old. I had just came back from Job Corps and moved in with a Foster Aunt named Minnie who already had 12 people living under her roof. I'm a grown ass woman who can't contribute anything financial, so I pay my way in sweat equity and tears. I became her workhorse. But when I showed her my pregnancy verification from Planned Parenthood the first words out her mouth were, "Hell Nawl. Yo ass can't stay here with no baby." She got too many mouths to feed as it is. I said ok and went in the room and lay on the floor dirty while she continued to go off, "Just cause you pregnant don't mean you get to lay up and do nothing, get yo ass up." It was only my slave ancestors that got me thru that difficult time. My girlfriend Tina told me about a shelter when she saw my hands elbow deep in suds washing dishes after 12 people and trying not to throw up in the sink. I found CASA in the yellow pages and made an appointment. Elaine interviewed me and after a week on the waiting list I was welcomed into the family.

I'm still blown away by the décor of the shelter. It's warm and inviting. My bedroom has a bed, a bassinet, a rocking chair and a little table and chair set to sit in. The colors are different in every room. I just feel like I'm going to be able to have a peaceful pregnancy here.

So, I'm in the sitting room that has books in it. I come here and sit on the recliner to read. Today I'm sitting, sipping on lemonade and reading my book and I look up and a girl says, "Oh I'm sorry, I didn't know anyone was here." Then she chuckled. I say, "No problem. I'm just reading." She walks off and I think to myself, oh a new girl. I need to find out who she is. I follow her and introduce myself, "Hi. I'm Peaches. She says, "I'm Jennifer." She's a petite girl with a big ole smile and a matching belly. I'm like, "Girl when your baby due?" She says, "February, you?" We instantly become friends and start sharing stories of our lives and sorry ass baby daddies. She got the same story we all have. One thing I like about her, she isn't afraid to express herself and she seem like she's gonna get her way no matter what. I wish I had her spunk.

CASA run's like a small community, maybe even a family. It's like a sanctuary for broken hearts. When I move in, they watch me drag my bags to the empty room that has been assigned to me. It's decorated in happy striped yellow wallpaper with little teddy bears painted on the crown molding that contrast my life. I don't even unpack. My bed is plush with a big cozy yellow comforter and soft pillows. There's a small sink in the corner. The sun shines through a picture window that looks out into a garden. I sit down with my 49ers jacket pulled tight around me and look around. There's no arguing, gunfire, shouting, fighting. It's quiet; blank space. I feel safe, I think. There's a tap at my door and before I can answer it's opening and Peaches is standing in the doorway, "We have circle time now."

I turn my nose up, "I'm cool."

She laughs, "Girl you have to come."

I'm thinking I don't have to do anything I don't want to do. She waves me on, "You might as well get used to it. Today is the first day of the rest of your life."

I can't help but laugh, "Yeah ok." I stand up and follow Peaches downstairs. All the other girls are gathering in the big living room with cups of hot chocolate like they are about to sing Christmas carols. I walk in slow trying to see what's up. I still have on my jacket. The other girls are watching me as I find a space beside Peaches. My attitude is strapped across my chest like a bullet proof vest. I barely nod when a few of the girls speak. I wonder which one I'm gonna have to chin check. In the center is a biracial lady with big curls. She tells me her name is Samantha. She looks kinda like Robin to me. She starts lighting candles. One of the girls cuts off the lights. I whisper to Peaches, "This some weird shit." She nods like she knows what I'm talkin about. In the dark words turn into a bonfire of sorrow. Cassie, a lanky cinnamon girl with a small tummy talks about letting three guys run a train on her at a motel, "I really just didn't care. Shoot I don't care bout this baby." Samantha asks if she thinks it's because of her past. She nods, "Probably." She says she buried her humiliation of past abuse in acid and crazy sexcapades. She likes to stay smelling good and looking good but deep down she's pushing up daisies from the past. The girls unleash some of the most terrible things I have ever heard of. I'm stunned. I find out that our pain is the ties that bind us.

My mother molested me. She used to fondle me when she was high on crack.

My boyfriend beat me unconscious while I was carrying his baby. I thought I was dead. I hoped I was.

A young Cuban girl named Damaris talks in a mambo Spanglish dialect and words dance around her tongue. She's from Florida and has been homeless ever since she moved to the Bay when her boyfriend was gone with the wind, leaving her in a city she knows nothing about. Tara a chalky charcoal skinned chick with rapid eye movements and potholes on her face. She's trying to kick a crack habit. She's 17. Shit like that. We just torn pages. Stories of broken promises, abandonment and depression unwind around me like a playlist of hopelessness. Peaches was born Heroine addicted and has been a foster child since her grandmother and aunt died months apart when she was 7 years old. The remaining family members ransacked the house and left her along with her baby brother waddling in shit. Her mother is still in Oakland somewhere getting high. At 20 she is an emancipated ward of the state but has nowhere to go. Tequila, a pretty black 18-year-old, has a keloided scar on her neck where her boyfriend has dragged a knife and slit her from ear to ear. She's ashamed and wears Muslim head wraps to cover the scars. She has another child who is a ward of the state. Their sadness mirrors mine. The first night I disappear in the room and just listen to their disappointments. I sit there speechless. I'm in a prison of uncertainty. They cry and hug each other. I'm crippled. The truth hurts too much. I guessed right, there ain't no unwed mothers in fairytales. I retreat to my room and my tears burn a hot trail into my pillow.

The next week I find my way back to the circle. I sit down in my donated flower summer dress and jean vest. I listen to other girls sharing their lives. How their family has pulled disappearing acts on them. I sit there in the circle again with a storm brewing inside me. Samantha tells me to unpack. Peaches is sitting beside me. We have become friends. She already knows why I'm here. She gives me a look that tells me to join in. It's like walking thru fire as I regurgitate my life. No one is shocked. They just listen. I tell them painfully about when I was a small child and my mother got so frustrated that's she hog tied me and taped my mouth with duct tape. I cried until snot ran from my nose onto the gray tape. When I talk about being molested, they don't flinch. Other girls joined in. Everyone in the room has experienced sexual abuse of some kind. The candle flames are dancing around in the darkness as we trade stories like trading cards, "But let me tell you what happened to me," Some stories are so vile that even us broken hearted girls get squeamish and hold our bellies. One girl talks about her Step-father raping her so many times that he impregnates her. Her mother then tries to fight the baby out of her. I'm sick to my stomach. I am amazed that these girls have survived so much and still have smiles on their faces. We blur into one. We hurt. We cry. We scars. We be the tears in the corner of your eyes.

Samantha smiles at me, "The good thing about rock bottom is there's nowhere else to go but up." I can feel my walls cracking, splintering and crashing to the floor like glass.

Just sharp edges

Broken

Into shards

PEACHES

CASA girls are very close to one another. We are all pregnant and in the same situation. We cook and eat together and sit on each other's beds and share stories. We walk up to Eastmont mall and have a sandwich or just hang out. One requirement of CASA is that you have to pay rent and give them all your food stamps. They make me go down to the County building to apply for welfare and give them $250.00 out of my $300 welfare check.

Two black women from a neighboring Baptist church come by and both hug me when they see me. They are smiling at my big stomach. They are so friendly. One of them smiles and says, "Honey, you are going to have everything you need for your baby, we went shopping and got many things for you guys and we cooked dinner for you too." They go outside and came back with long aluminum pans filled with green beans, mashed potatoes, corn, gravy. My hungry ass is like shit, we hit the jackpot! They put the food on the table and leave. I run to get the other girls. When I come back and grab a plate, one of the red-faced nuns stops me, 'This food is not for you. We're taking this to a homeless shelter." I Stand holding my plate hot as fish grease, "What are we? Aren't we homeless?" I hate this place.

I'm playing music on the stereo in the hall, *U.N.I.T.Y., Love a black woman from (You got to let him know) infinity to infinity-Queen Latifah (U.N.I.T.Y.)*

I drag the yellow mop bucket down the long hall, lift the mop, pull the handle to wring it out and slosh the gray strings on the wooden floor in the dining room with an attitude. Tara is pulling the vacuum down the long-carpeted hallways with a grudge. Damaris is indignant on her knees in the bathroom scrubbing the floor tiles cussing in Spanish. I'm annoyed that Peaches has kitchen duties. It's always the easiest. She's smiling and chopping carrots to add to the fresh vegetable salad she's making. We can only cook nutritious meals. Christmas music is playing. Other girls are setting the long dining room table for our 6 o'clock dinner. We all have to eat dinner together at the designated dinner time.

I look at the red marks on my fingers from the sewing needle and get mad. I've made as many receiving blankets and baby crib stuff than I can stand. I've sewn pillows, diaper stackers and bibs all with the same choo-choo train pattern for the little boy I discovered I'm having. I feel like CASA has turned into a slave ship and Elaine is the Master. I'm not use to all these chores and structure. Everything has a time and an order. We complain day in and day out to the nuns, but they rule the nest with strict principles. I even try to get my doctor to sign off and say a pregnant woman can't work this hard. They won't.

I beg Elaine to let me stay in the bed when the therapist visits or when we have workshops. An artist volunteers to give us art therapy where we are encouraged to paint new pictures of our lives. Volunteer nurses give us birthing classes and domestic skills training. I try to stay woke while a lady stands with a projector and talks about the female anatomy and what to expect in labor, "When your mucus plug comes out contractions should start..." They assign me a midwife and she coaches me on my labor. I get a milkmaid who shows me how to make a baby "latch-on." It's information overload and I am getting so big and tired and all I want to do is sleep. But they keep coaching me like I'm a fighter in a boxing ring. "Get up," "Keep swinging." I just want to sleep.

The few friends I call, I have to call at an allotted time and sit in a smelly old pine wood phone booth box that smells like spit. The whole time you talk other girls beat on the door. I open the door and square up on a broad, "Wait damn!" You can take the girl out the hood but best believe the hood is still in this girl. I call my mom to let her know where I am. I dial her number and as it rings, I feel a tingling in my belly. I hadn't talked to her since the panty incident. I know she doesn't recognize the number but as it rings for a while, I hope she answers anyway. She answers in her usual exhausted tone, "Hello." I can picture her laying across her bed in the dark with a migraine.
I pause for a moment. Then I nervously run it to her, "Mom I'm just letting you know I'm in a shelter."
She sighs in relief when she hears my voice, "Oh ok."
"I just wanted you to know."
There's silence for a moment like neither of us know what to say.
Then she says, "I'm glad you are somewhere safe."
I laugh a little, 'Yeah I guess you can say that. I'm on a slave ship."
She laughs. It's good to hear her smile through the phone.
She giggles when I tell her about all the coaching and the sewing and worst of all the chores.
She sounds tired. I ask her if she's ok. "Well I am making it."
"Well I'm having a boy."
She laughs, "Oh a big head boy huh."
"Yep. I am going to name him Khali."
"That's a nice name."
"Yeah it's Arabic it mean's friend of Allah."
"Oh ok."
Our conversation is brief, but its impact is long-lasting.

PEACHES

Do Ms. Peaches got to rob a bitch? It's do or die day, in other words, "Merry Christmas." I'm disappointed by the lack of gifts for my baby. This shelter has taken all the gifts hostage. They gave me two gifts; a pink crochet blanket and a cotton sweat suit. Jennifer has a wicked smile on her face and her eyes meet mine. I smile back. I don't know what you gone do but I already know what I'm about to do. I call my baby daddy first. I tell him I really need help. His response? "I ain't gotta buy the baby shit." I must be in the twilight zone. "Excuse me?" *Did this motherfucker just say he not gonna help me with this baby?* He says, "You heard me. I ain't got to help you with shit, as a matter of fact, I ain't got to do shit for you or that baby until the baby is born." SLAP. I just got slapped in my face with a dose of fucked-up-ness. Now my head is reeling. I am sitting in this little ass phone booth getting told by my child's father that he is not going to help me with a child he begged me to have. Thoughts are going thru my head fast.

No money, no Christmas gifts, no family, no love, no future, no life, no, no, noooo. After my mental spiral, I quickly recover, "Cool." Click. He tries to say something as I slam down the phone. I won't speak to him until after the baby is born. I don't have no use for a never-have-a-penny-ass-nigga.

I sit in my room and rock in my rocking chair. I made up my mind. I'm robbing the Chapel. When everyone goes to sleep, I'm going to the chapel and taking everything, I want. I made up my mind that they are all some fake ass prejudice nuns. They aren't going to play me.

Jennifer and I creep down the stairs. Samantha says she's gonna turn her back and not see anything. I walk in with garbage bags. We pick the lock. The door burst open. My eyes get big as saucers when I see all that stuff. I get pissed instantly. *Ain't this a bitch.* They got all this stuff an ain't gonna give it to us? I pick up everything I think my baby needs; dresses, sleepers, baby magic lotion, wash clothes, socks, baby shoes, clothes, diapers, teething rings, whatever. I'm on a shopping spree. I look over at Jennifer. I say, "Girl grab something for your baby." Jennifer says, "No Peaches you taking too much. They are gonna know." I whisper back, "I don't give a fuck if they know. "Girl get some stuff." I was furious. Jennifer's eyes are darting all around. I say "Ok, ok. I'll stop." I grab my bags full of baby stuff and throw them over my shoulder. Jennifer bust out laughing, "Yo ass look like Santa Claus." My friend DeeDee is my getaway driver. I run to the front door, throw the bag in the car and run back to CASA.

Peaches is starting to act out. She's feeling held captive by too many rules and regulations. She has come from a foster care and group homes and rules only remind her of the hard days and unfair treatment she's suffered at the hands of folks who claim to be helping her. She's been abused by too many homes. Thanksgiving comes and goes, and I volunteer to help pack donated gifts to hand out in the community. I tell Peaches we have stashed them in the Cathedral that's beside the shelter. She decides she's going to rob them. I'm a thief at heart but I secretly have started to like Elaine and the nuns at CASA, but loyalty runs deep in my veins like red Kool-Aid. So, when Peaches gears up to make the heist, I'm on all fours picking the lock of the Cathedral like the professional I am. But when I shimmy the doors open and thrust on the lights and see bookoos of merchandise all over the floor of the church, I freeze up. I watch Peaches run around grabbing stuff, filling up her black hefty bag and tossing it over her shoulder like she's Santa. I stand motionless at the door and for the first time, I can't bring myself to steal. I back out and wait until she's done. Even when they interrogate me, I keep my vow of silence. But this marks the beginning of the end for Peaches and CASA. She decides to take her chances on the street. I wave her goodbye and wait out my pregnancy.

24: The birth of the blues.

Elaine comes with me to court when I go to report on my probation. She vouches for me. She sits in the court with me and tells the judge that I am living in a shelter and working to better myself. While I stand there with a lump in my throat, she vouches for my work with her and the other Sisters and says that I am fulfilling my community service. This is the first time that anyone has come to court with me. It's because of her that I don't get remanded into custody for missing court dates while I was looking for a place to live.

After we leave she takes me to a small Café in Berkeley North of Shattuck Ave. in what we call the *Gourmet ghetto* and she orders me a spiced black tea with milk while we sit on the patio in the cool air and watch the hippies walk by in sandals and ankle length bohemian skirts. A long-haired white guy zips by on his bike past vender booths where artist sell their handcrafted goods. I like the Tie dye shirts, Hemp flip flops and African jewelry. I buy a shell necklace for $2.00. We sip tea against the backdrop of UC Berkeley's campus. Black college boys stand in front of "Fat Slice" pizzeria munching on big slices of pepperoni Pizza dripping with cheese. I'm 9 months pregnant now and my belly is the biggest thing on my small body. I've slipped my swollen ankles into some comfy Birkenstocks. Elaine is smiling at me softly like she wants to ask me something. I roll my eyes, 'What?" She shrugs shyly and ask, "How does it feel to be a mother?" I shrug, like I know. It dawns on me that she doesn't either. She's a forty-something year old lady that has probably never even had sex. Here she is sitting across the table from a young black teen about to have a baby. She folds her napkin like she always does across her lap gently, "I admire your strength. You don't seem to be afraid. It would terrify me." I don't know how to be fragile and soft. I sure don't know how to be afraid. She tells me I can find a job cleaning some houses of a few white people she knows. I shrug. It sounds good.

It's storming and hailing outside when my water breaks. The other girls crowd in the bathroom stalls watching me stand with my underwear on my ankles and thick mucus sliding down my legs. The dam has been breached and my uterus unleashed its waters all at once. I rush from the stall, almost tripping over myself and grab the phone to call my midwife. I pace the long hallways with wide-eyed girls standing in their doorways while my contractions wring piss out my uterus with each pang. I forget to count the intervals. The contractions are crashing into each other like waves crashing into the shore. They all seem less than five minutes apart. I call my mom, 'I'm going in labor!" I take a shower because I don't want my coochie to be funky. In the shower my stomach wretches into knots and blood runs down the drain. Samantha swings the van around and me, her and Tequila jump into the Van and head to Berkeley medical center. I start vomiting in the vehicle and my contractions are strong and barely let up.

By the time I make it I've dilated a lot. I'm puking and trembling and wobbling to the entrance. My mom is in the emergency room looking more nervous than me. By the time I make it to labor and delivery I'm worn out from the contractions and my body is cold. I lay in the stirrups with blood staining my thighs. I have to shit. I tell my mom, "I feel rigor mortis setting in." She laughs. I'm serious though, my shoulders are going stiff. My midwife rushes in and starts massaging me. The doctor wants to cut me. She's already coached me on what to say. I tell the doctors I want her to deliver my baby. She slides in a stool between my legs and starts rubbing my cervix with oils. I'm delirious. I'm hurting. It's blinding pain. I want the Epidural. I grab my IV and strain my neck to see if I see the epidural man. She's soothing me with her words of comfort. I'm writhing in pain, losing time. She tells me to match her breathing. I do. The nurses are all gathering around to see what teenage pregnancy looks like on me. My mother is stroking my arms and hair. I don't want to have a baby. Now his head has burrowed into my pelvis sending shooting pains into my backbone. The midwife is back between my legs massaging the pain and suddenly his little head crowns. When she lifts her hands up in the air, I see a pale wide mouthed infant with eyes slanted like mine and silky hair. I draw back a little, *what the*...My mom squeals, "He's beautiful Nise." I don't know about that. I look at the wormish squirming guy whose been imprisoned between my rib cage for 9 months. He's pasty but not bloody. His white skin is wrinkled and scaly like a lizard. She lays him in my shaking arms and turns his face to my titty. He's licking his lips and sucking awkwardly at first but after a minute he locks on like a pit-bull, suctioning milk as he nurses for the first time. My mom is tearing up as she watches me feed him. I'm just watching my son and he's watching me. I can't believe I'm his mother. The first night when we are alone, I just lay watching him sleep starring at the blue veins in his face. I look at his tiny legs and little body. My life ain't never been no place for a kid. I wonder how I can take care of him for 18 years. Worry creeps up beside me. I'm afraid. I'm alone and I'm homeless.

I bring my bundle of joy to CASA and a dozen young women are standing waiting to welcome him into our family. I'm the first to give birth. Everyone is so excited for me. I'm just tired. I sit on the armchair and they surround me while I peel back his covers like rose petals. 'He's so beautiful." "He's so tiny." "He's so yellow." Elaine watches me bathe him. I see admiration in her face. Now I know why she does this for us. She loves motherhood. She watches me feed him and she compliments me on my nurturing skills, "You are so good at this." I guess I am.

I have my new son Khali strapped to my chest in a snuggly, his little legs dangling, while I'm on the bus. Nobody offers up a seat, so I balance 7 pounds of baby weight on my 125-pound frame like an old pro. A lady across from me is cutting her eyes at me. I'm another young black single mother whose welfare is coming out of her paycheck. Medicaid and Wic don't compensate for the last few nights I've spent stone faced with my baby's cries echoing into the emptiness in my head wanting to toss him from the rocking chair into the wall. Food stamps don't bring his daddy over to visit. Medi-CAL doesn't quiet the madness of my thoughts. My body is still aching from labor, but the welfare office makes you come and reapply for your assistance within a week of giving birth or risk losing your stamps. I had a baby, but it seems I gave birth to heartache and pain. Nobody explained to me the strangling emotions you experience after birth, when all the visitors leave you to the chaos of motherhood. The nurses mention the tearing and ripping of your vagina and hand me a spray bottle to ease the burning when I piss. But what about the stabbing pains in my heart when his father makes excuses when I ask for money? I look into Khali's eyes as the bus rounds McArthur Blvd. My coochie aches from having just given birth. He looks up and smiles with his eyes. I touch his nose and he makes his noises. I lean on the metal pole and watch him watching me and I realize that I have become somebody. I start seeing myself in his eyes. I start hearing myself in his laughter. When he smiles at me, I feel big. The bus stops and the world moves around me but I have let down my anchor and now the storms inside me are still. A man bumps me as he passes, "You have a cute baby." I do.

Tequila's father visits CASA. He's a pastor of a small church in West Oakland. I start going to church service with her. He sings, "I want to go home." So beautifully that we are all in tears. Home is a place I long for also. After service he tells his daughter that he has talked a friend of his name Reverend Blackmon into letting her and her kids stay in an apartment that he owns. But Tequila has decided to leave CASA and return to her abusive relationship. She turns it down. Without hesitation he offers it to me. I'm dumfounded at his kindness.

25: How to build a fire. The trouble with

Tequilla is that she has no imagination. But I have an over-active mind. I invent my reality every day. Even though I can't see myself being successful, hope is a light house in my dark and foggy thoughts. I must really be crazy like my mother always tells everybody. I always jump off the cliff and let chance build wings before I hit the ground.

I drag a military duffle bag full of my things with Khali in a hiking carrier on my back to the raggedy two-bedroom apartment on the edge of a busy intersection in China Town. A Chinaman stares from the window in the next building as I beat on the door. The apartment sits smack dab in the middle of the hoe-stroll E14th. I ain't traveling alone though, I picked up a stray. A 17-year-old project princess named Michelle struggled to keep up with me carrying a Hefty bag of clothes and a heavy emotional load on her small shoulders after her boyfriend 86'd her.

MICHELLE

I leave a bag of old clothes blowing in the wind near the phone booth. Jennifer tells me less is more. I just met her at a payphone downtown. I been kicked to the curb, literally. I was on the payphone begging my 18-year-old boyfriend to let me stay with him and his mom. My mom is probably in a dope house in Cypress Village somewhere overdosing on reality. I've been sitting here since the bus driver pulled the levee and shut the door when I told him I only had 50 cents on me, but I wanted to go to West Oakland to look for my mom. I guess I underestimated the coldness of the human heart. Not given a shit is at an all-time high these days. I can't believe he is screaming at me from the other side, "Fuck you bitch. I told you I didn't want the baby." I'm 17 and pregnant with his child. I didn't do this alone. I know he's afraid of what his mom is gonna say if she knows I'm three months pregnant. But I want him to man-up. He got amnesia now all of a sudden. I'm crying my eyes out holding onto Safeway bags with my clothes in it. People are walking by like I'm invisible, trying not to see me. This girl with a baby stops and ask me what's wrong. She heard me going off on my dude. I don't know this girl, but I need someone, anyone. I unload everything I been going through and she doesn't flinch. She isn't smiling. She looks tired and irritated, but I think she understands.

Michelle's eyes are thin layers of ice and when the bough breaks, she gives way to relentless tears. I know, I know...*it's raining it's pouring...* I was too tired to sing a long, but I couldn't leave her crying. She latched onto me like a life raft. "I ain't got nowhere to go." *Join the crowd.* I rolled my eyes, "I got a place." *Rise sally Rise. Wipe your weepin eyes.* She better tighten the straps on her bra and keep pushing. A girl can't afford to be weak. I picked her up like the lost and found girl I once was. My mom said I always brought home strays; cats, puppies, kids. I tell her to leave a bag so she can keep up with my pace. I can't explain or offer her any pity. Ain't no rhythm to these blues, just a steady beat that presses you forward. She's sad saying, "He hung up on me." *I know the story already, Georgie Porgies' pudding pie, kissed the girls and made them cry.* Shit doesn't even matter to me anymore.
I walked on down the hill and like Jill she came tumbling after.

Now we both stand in the doorway of a dusty duplex with paint peeling from the wood, broken windows and a patchwork of soiled carpet and I think about Langston Hughes poem I memorized in 7th grade English.
Well son, life for me ain't been no Crystal Stair...It's had tacks in it
 with splinters
and boards torn up
The previous tenant had left two couches, an old handmade wooden TV stand and a small TV. I pointed to the love seat, "You sleep on that one." Michelle collapses on it. I plop down on the big couch and took Khali out of the metal carrier. He giggled and fell into the dingy sofa cushions and started reaching in my shirt for my breast. I whipped out my breast and let him hungrily suck

the life out of me. Not eating and breastfeeding was causing me to lose too much weight. But *I'se been a-climbin' on.*

I hear a tap on the door and looked back to see a short man in wife beater and black slacks with a simple cross on his neck, "How you doing? Which one of you is Jennifer?" I pulled my shirt over Khali's head, "I am." He looks me over then back at Michele resting her tired feet on the arm of the couch, "I'm Reverend Blackmon. I only have two rules, have my money by the 1st and don't have no men in here." He starts to walk off then turned back, "Oh and y'all can have this stuff here. I ain't got no use for it." When he closes the door, I looked back at Michelle and she squeals, "Damn he fine."

He wasn't only fine, but he was a handy man. Almost a month later he was on our kitchen floor on his back with his arms bulging twisting a wrench under our sink to stop the sink from dripping all night. Me and Michelle stood over him watching him work. Khali was climbing over his tools getting in the way. Rev. Blackmon reached for a screwdriver. He had made a small attempt at dating me, but I declined. I think He's out of my league. Attending a Fashion show seemed far-fetched. But I'm rethinking it now watching him under my sink. He looks up at me with soft eyes and asks, "You got my money yet Girl?" "Nope."

But I was on it. Even hell hath no fury like a woman standing on her last dollar. I knew he'd take a couchie coupon, but I wasn't going out like that. Michelle was like a motherless child herself and was looking to me for nurturing. I roll my eyes at her. I'm bleeding out from trying to keep diapers on my son and food in all our mouths. Michelle doesn't have the street instincts that I do. She worries about childish things like not getting her nails done while I pillage for tissue and deodorant. She doesn't know how to steal, how to hustle niggas, or anything else of street value. We're living an imitation of life as a family and she's the teenage daughter of a teenage daughter. I need help. I have to locate my partner in crime, Peaches. Last I heard she had been living in the Acorn projects for a while after she left CASA. I track her down to her baby father's house on Fruitvale where she's sleeping on the couch with their newborn while he and his current girlfriend took the bedroom. It was an uncomfortable situation to say the least. While Jerry Blackmon laid on the floor fixing our sink, I place a call to my old buddy. Peaches is the only one I know can come up with some money by any means necessary.

"I need some money with the quickness."
She blows hot air into the phone, "I feel you. I got to get out of June bugs house. But I ain't got shit."
I'm in a bind. "I need $600 dollars." I lower my voice, "I ain't got no rent money. We're gonna get put out." I'm riding on fumes and Jerry Blackmon's desire for me. I might have to pay in sweat equity.
She's down like four flats, "I'll get three, you get three."
"Bet."
She's ten-toes down. An hour later she's on the dirty ass carpet with me placing calls like a call-a-thon to every negro we knew in the East bay who has a few dollars to throw around.
"Hey Yusef, what you up to? I know it's been a minute. I been going through some shit. Check this out-you got 100?"
"A hundred dollars? Hell naw." He just had a son himself and he was selling incense at the Bart Station to make money.
"I need some rent money or it's over for me."
"I got $50 on it."
"Bet."
I hit my other homies pager. He rings back.
"Hey Maceo. I need a favor..."
She calls old boy and whathisface she grew up with. She hits up 50-dollar Craig and 25-dollar Antwan.
By the break of dawn, we got 600 hundred dollars pieced together from beg and borrowed hopes, wishes of friends and from strong-arming guys emotions.
Now there are three of us living on two couches in a rundown

134

apartment in China Town. Khali is snoring on my chest on the love seat, Delores is snuggled up with her daughter on the sofa and Michele is taking up space on the floor. You gotta earn the couch. Together we have about 50 dollars in food stamps and some Boonsfarm to warm up with.

After the phone gets cut off, I have to walk to the pay phone at the corner to place calls while watching the 57 passes by blowing black clouds of smoke on the half hour. I got my back to traffic, balancing Khali in his backpack carrier trying to ignore the guys circling in their cars like sharks honking at me and yelling out of the window, "Aye mama you want a date for 40 dollars?" *40 dollars?* My blood boils. That's hoe terminology for let me buy some ass. I guess sex is cheap these days. I ain't got a good time for sale and 40 dollars ain't gonna buy them a kiss on the forehead.

I lean on the metal box and look at a woman whose hips are swinging to the rhythm of the dope fiend. Her heavy switch and butt cheeks hanging out her skirt let me know she's working the stroll. I see them all day passing in front of my window like phantoms. *Let's get the rhythm of the head, ding dong.* She's walking and waving a car to the corner, *Shimmy, Shimmy cocoa pop, Shimmy, Shimmy pow.* When she passes me, our eyes connect for a brief moment and time slows to a halt. I remember a pretty golden skinned girl with dimples with that same dangerously sexy swing to her hips. I see a split second of recognition in her eyes before she looks off. I don't even hear that my call has been answered because I'm so shocked at her scorched skin, rail thin legs and the skeletal face with sunken in dimples. I want to call out to her but the way she looked right through me; I know that she doesn't want me to see her. We both act like we don't. But I know those hazel eyes. *Damn Queen.* I want to put my arms around Delana's little sister and pull her into the refuge of our place on E14th, but I know she wants to stay invisible. I want to kiss the bones on her cheek. I just watch her pass to the corner and slip into a burgundy Buick.

I get home and throw myself on the couch next to Maceo, "I got to get out of Oakland." He puts his Glock on the table and lays back with his head in my breast. I adore him. We watch my son playing on the floor with Peaches daughter and Yusef's thumb sucking son. Tia's in the doorway stirring a mixing bowl of Jiffy cornbread. Her belly is big with her second baby. She lives around the corner in a condemned house that her baby daddy sells crack out of. She serves his dope too and keeps a shotgun behind the door in case anyone tries to run off with her man's shit. The problem is, his mom's a fiend and she cuffs more than he can sell. Tia comes to our place every day because they don't have running water and no refrigerator. We merge our money and stamps and cook every single day. CASA got me and Peaches into preparing meals, so we cut up carrots and potatoes every day and feed the multitude their daily bread while listening to ghetto classics on the tape deck.

Now Maceo's laying on my chest full as a tick with half his hair braided into a corn roll and the other half wild as he is. I shake him, "Are you going to bring me a bed?"
I'm tired of sleeping on the hard ass couch. He smirks that same ol cocky smile, "You gone give me some?"
"Boy quit." We all laugh at his roguishness. He got jokes. He pops my titty, "Actually, I'm glad you never gave me none." He gets quiet for a moment then looks up at me and acknowledges, "Cause if you did, we probably wouldn't have this." I think about his statement.
This...shabby apartment with the fucked-up carpet on the corner of E14th street where the sun don't shine.
This strip where prostitute's step off the sidewalk into economy cars,
where Peaches got chicken wings poppin in grease
where Tia makes the cornbread in a gas oven while cooking up ideas of motherhood and womanliness and feeding man boys who hunger for dignity and worth and that they might be missed someday by somebody, somewhere.

This is where Michelle dries her panties on the heater cause we don't have a washer or dryer. This is the only place where Yusef feels safe dropping off his son because his mentally ill wife can't keep him.

Here, where Suinjata rolls up, dragging his ten-speed into the kitchen before he falls asleep in a corner on Khali's baby crib mattress.

Where Maceo comes after doing his dirt and feels safe enough to take the gun off his waistband and kick back on my tit.

This is where Amini feeling fried, dyed and laid to the side, can swing through after she leaves beauty school and get a hot meal.

This is where Jbird pulls up incognegro in his cocaine white Benz, but I decide that I'd rather ride with the ones who love me.

This is family.

These four little walls frame a jig-saw puzzle of kinfolk. We gather in the living room and warm ourselves by the fire of friendship.

This is my tribe.

These broken pieces that somehow fit together.

This is home.

Where we share stories of death.

Births.

Love unrequited.

Coversatin'

And ghetto politickin'

Where I make playlist of laughter, and joy and quiet sobs in the pillow beneath my tangled blinds.

This little corner of our world -where we set the night to Maxwell's Ascension tape, belly laughs and swirling Nag Champa incense smoke.

"Shouldn't I realize, you're the highest of the high. If you don't know then I'll say it, so don't ever wonder,"

26: Hood-Rat

Hood-rat. It's 1996, The year of the rat. Hood rat is a common term used to refer to chicks who have the unfortunate luck of being born and raised in the slums. She's said to be a young promiscuous woman who lives in a poor urban area and like a rodent gnaws on all the resources but doesn't add any value to the landscape. But the funny thing is that in some culture's rats are mythical creatures, they are quick-witted, resourceful and versatile. They have strong intuition and quick reflexes, and always adapt themselves to new environments.

But this is Oakland. In the ghetto a rat wears neon spandex from Rainbow fashions, has Kim-Lee paint garnet red on her artificial nails and has hair styled by home-girl kitchen beauticians. She is said to be uneducated and according to urban mythology doesn't want anything else in life other than some good weed and a good time. In the Chinese calendar- 1996 is the year of the rat. We ghetto girls walk the six blocks from Lucky's balancing grocery bags on our cheap strollers like beast of burden while guys shake their heads at us. We around-the-way-girls. Our very presence brings the property value down. I peel food stamps out of a book of stamps at Safeway and sting with shame as working-class women comment to each other, "Some of us have to work to buy food." We roll our hips in the living room, dancing ourselves dizzy to 2 Live Crew screaming, "Hoodrat, Hoodrat Hoochie mama, you ain't nothing but a Hoochie mama."

We sit on our stoop abandoned like yesterday's trash waiting to be picked up and carried off. We spend our days drinking, cussing, sleeping, eating and raging against the dying of our spirits. We sit and simmer with maddening poverty. We eat it. We drink it. We shake it down our hips. We are the reapers of smirks and cruel eyes burning with judgment. We dried up roses. We die in the eyes of strangers, every day, 10 times a day. We cut our eyes and flash our teeth at whoever wants it. We are the loveless; the ones that love just couldn't protect. Love couldn't convince. Love couldn't comfort on colds nights. Love damn sure can't bring daddies to the side of our babies' cribs. Now the cat calls from young hustlers have turned into insults from dirty old dried out cat daddies. Now the fog of gin and weed has cleared and the aftertaste is sickening. This the junkyard of old ride or dies after the chop shop has stripped all the good stuff. When you try to make a life out of fractions; pieces of a whole. Garbage men visit us at night, hit us like freak accidents and pass judgment just as quick as they pull up their Levi's in the morning.

This is the other side of the game, when all the lip gloss dries up on your lips and the eyeliner has been cried off your bottom lash. This where the sun don't shine. On this stoop, the cheap smell of dime store body spray mixes with piss and the funky fumes of despair. It seems I've given up the drive byers and kick door burglars of West Oakland for the sex traps and dope alleys on the East. At night I lay in my bed and try to tune out the honking cars, growling buses and screaming women. I try to block out the negative thoughts spilling over from the toxic wasteland of my mind. I want to float out this black hole. I spend almost a year on the couch waiting for the world to change. Thinking of all the guys who used me, tripping over cupids broken arrows and tuning life out. I'm disgusted in what I've turned out to be. I hear Charles' words on my conscience, *most likely to be a prostitute*.

This is the year I find myself trapped inside myself. I'm Anony-Miss. Miss-understood. Miss-taken identity. Every time I get up and look in the mirror, I see a hood rat, a ghetto chick, a young hoochie. The sofa, the floor, the windows, everything I look at is grey and dingy as despair. I see my yearbook photo with "Most Attractive," and I think about all the guys shouting to me as I walk around Lake Merritt in my half shirt and cut-offs going to the grocery store. I don't know if I have anything else good about me. I pass in front of stores window shopping with dark circles under my eyes and know that I still can't afford anything in there. Every month I spend whatever I have left from my welfare check on a pair of baby Jordan's, or a $12 Nike hat, or knock-off Fila shirt for my son so that when we stand at the bus stop and when people see him they say, "Now she takes care of her boy." I'm emotionally broke. He's all I have in the form of wealth. He's my billboard. I stand still with my son waiting on the 72 while the earth rotates without me.

I spend days wallowing in self-pity and nights stumbling over my thoughts. I'm used to being depressed. But it's more than that, the sky is falling. I reach out to my mom and find out from Tim that she has left the State. She ran for her life to little Rock, Arkansas leaving everything she owned, including me. Again.
On September 13th I'm standing by the sofa talking to Peaches when we barely hear a newscaster interrupt the regular programming, "Rapper Tupac Shakur has died as result of his injuries from the September 7th shooting in Las Vegas..." *wait what?* I sink. We all just kind of standstill in a moment of stunned silence while the world continues to turn. Tia rounds the corner. Just that fast, the TV returns to its program. We all just look at each other. No way. The city of Oakland is shell-shocked from the news. The radio stations play all day tributes to our fallen hero and people call in the hotline to voice their hurt, anger and frustration at the loss of our brother. Store fronts are plastered with Tupac posters, flags and any memorabilia. It's a solemn time in Oakland, the whole city is crying. At least he's away from here.

27: **Building Bridges**

I'm walking from downtown Oakland in the shadow of the Bay Bridge. I slip into Laney Community College and walk around campus. I have a bench warrant for failure to appear and I need to enroll in somebodies school to show father judge I'm productive. I want to disappear in the crowd of young minds rushing to and from classes like they are in a hurry to be somebody. But I only exist inside statistics, on court dockets and case numbers. I live on waiting list and kept alive by data. I'm wandering aimlessly watching the young women lit with ambition exchanging ideas or connecting over Iced lattes. I look lost. A girl my age smiles at my baby attached to my chest in his snuggly. A guy in a baseball cap tells me to go to Admissions. He points at a triangular white concrete building.

I cut across the greenery and go to where he said "Admissions" is at and ask what it would would take to enroll. I'm standing at the counter in booty shorts and Timberland boots with Khali strapped to my chest feeling my way thru the darkness while a lady at the counter stares at me coldly while she instructs me, "fill out the admissions packet and get a FASFA application." I don't know what it's for, but I answer the questions about my income with ease. I don't have none, nada, zilch. I get a welfare check for $600 a month, a handful of WIC vouchers and $300 dollars in Food stamps. "Now what?" I ask. She asks me what I want to Major in. I'm confused. I don't know what that means. She breaks it down, "What do you want to go to school to become?"
I shrug my shoulders. I don't know. I figured I'd just wing it like I usually do.
She's irritated by my attitude, "Why do you want to go to school?"
Cause Boys go to Jupiter to get stupider. But *Girls go to college to get more knowledge.* I shrug.

She shakes her head and lowers me a rope, "What are you good at?"

Stealing. "Nothing."

She looks at my FASFA and frowns, "We'll call you when it goes through."

I just shake my head, "Ok."

"What's your phone number?"

I answer without blinking, "I ain't got no phone. I use the payphone on E14th." The hoe stroll.

She looks at me astonished, "You don't have a phone?"

I want to say, Ma'am, I ain't got shit. I shrug my shoulders, "I'll just come back and check on it." She pulls out a book of checks and starts filling one out, "Get you a phone. You ain't got no business using the payphone on *that* street." Bitch I live on *that* street. She rips the check out and hands it to me. The check is for $300. I'm stunned. She smiles, "This is an advance on your Pell. If you come back, we can waive your tuition. The State of California waves the tuition for Single mothers." She says, "You can also get a book grant to cover other cost." *Grant? Is that money?*

I sit on the couch at home and still in a state of shock relay it to Peaches., "I think I'm going to college."

She's bathing her daughter in a baby tub on our dirty carpet, "That's cool. You think you'll get accepted?"

I really don't know. I thought only rich kids who had parents that saved for their kids' college tuition were able to go. I think about the boys I saw outside of Fat Slice in Berkeley. The girls I saw at Laney bouncing with determination. my GPA is a 1.5. I shrug, I don't know what the fuck that means. "I don't know but they gave me some money." I show Peaches my check. We both laugh. School might just be my next hustle.

I go to Laney and check to see if I see my name on the list posted on the wall in the financial aid office. There are hundreds of names on the list. I come every week and never see my name. But this day I'm browsing the "T's" and my eyes screech to a halt. *It's here.* My name is on the list! I want to jump up and down. I go to the window. "My name is on there!" There's another lady there now. She's looking me up in the computer while I try to steady myself. Khali is resting quietly on my chest. It's taking too long. I think it may be a mistake. But when she looks up and smiles my heart skips, "You have been approved." She hands me a sheet of paper. You will receive a refund in a little while. But for now, you'll need to register for your classes."

I sit in the advisor's office bouncing Khali on my leg while he has head under my shirt breastfeeding. I tell the advisor I have never been to college. She's an Asian lady typing with small hands.

She asks, "How old is your baby.

I tell her, "Khali is one." His chunky legs kick around while he feeds.

She laughs, 'My goodness he's bigger than you."

I laugh too.

She asks me about my High school grades.

I tell her the truth, 'I'm not good at Math. I can write though. I read."

She types for a minute and says, "I recommend you for our Bridge program. That's a program that will help bridge you to the college life. It will help you become proficient enough to pass college level courses."

I shrug. I don't care. I just want to go to school. Ever since the lady in admissions told me I could go it sparked a flame inside me. Now I'm on fire for this school thing. She links me to the program that's supposed to help me become a successful student.

The first day in Bridge I don't know what to expect. Peaches gave me a tablet to write on. I have a pen and yes, I have Khali strapped to my chest like a baby Kangaroo. I sit in the back of the class with a blanket over my shoulder and listen and take notes and occasionally breast feed. The class is full of ex-military vets, recovering addicts and juvenile delinquents. I guess I fit in. It's a program where you have all your classes in one little area of the campus. We rotate about three classrooms a day taking all our general education classes together as a group. I sit in class and watch some white teacher write a list of words on the board. She writes the first one neatly, *Epitome*.

She puts the chalk down and turns to her class, "Who can tell me what this word means?" No one answers.

I look around, *are you serious?* I raise my hand, "to embody something."

Her eyes light up, "Yes!"

Everyone focuses on me. I do the next word, *persevere* "to do it in spite of it being difficult." I go down the whole list, my mind opens like a vault of information. I've read the *Autobiography of Malcolm X* twice, Alex Haley's *Roots, Nathan McCall's makes me wanna holla, Richard Wright's Native Son, Maya Angelou, I know why the caged bird sings....* The pages of my mind burst open like a library. A concealed weapon. My vocabulary is impeccable-*flawless; faultless*. Words are like flowers that blossom all around me. She smiles, "What's your name Sweetie?" I'm embarrassed, "Jennifer." After class a military Vet approaches me. He's a 30 something year old guy who left the military and got hooked on dope. He looks at me in amazement, "You're pretty smart huh?" His words breathe into me filling me with pride. I shrug, "I guess so." I guess so because when the grades are posted I have straight As. I look at the sheet of paper dumfounded. I have never ever ever in my long-legged life had grades like this assigned to me. I float down a river of words, past the street soldiers, passing the whores, bypassing the beggars. I run home to show Peaches.

Peaches is in the living room ironing the wrinkles out of a big mammy dress. She has been going out every day, catching the bus with her daughter, looking for a job. She has been told no in ten different ways, *we're sorry but you have no experience* and *I was looking for someone with a little more work history* or *We just filled the position.* I sit behind her and let Khali out of his carrier. She barely looks up, "I got an interview at some alarm place.

It pay $5 an hour."

I lay back on the sofa,

"I hope you get it."

"Me too shit."

We now have two more girls living with us. Some chicks Peaches knows from Acorn projects. They don't help us pay anything, they don't baby sit or do anything else worthwhile they just gather in our home seeking refuge from the storm of their lives. Peaches feels a certain loyalty to them because while she was in foster care, they took to her like family. Now we have females crashing in every nook and cranny in our house but not a spare nickel to rub together between us all. I still dump over couch cushions looking for change to buy toilet paper. I'm still feeding Khali and Michelle on a ramen noodle budget. It seems like all we ever got is excuses and not enough answers to go around. I can't have this. I can't do that. The pressure of everything is breaking Peaches' back too. Every day she battles with hope dangling like the panties and bras hanging from the shower rod in our bathroom or dreams scattered like the cheap make-up that covers the sink. She leaves the house at 5am, walking the rubber off her Payless dress shoes for a job that she never gets. She's complaining every day, *my back hurt, my bra too tight, my booty shaking from the left to the right.*

I lay my grades on the ironing board and see her face break into a smile, "You go girl." Peaches is a few years older than me and proud of me like I'm her baby girl. She laughs, "You a smarty art nigga." I wag my behind, "Yep," strutting like a peacock.

Get it girl!

But then the bottom falls out. My dreams are cut short the first day of the new semester. I think I got this school thang down now. I'm toting Khali as usual, but I don't make it past the entrance. The instructor is standing in the doorway with her nose turned up, "Jennifer we can't allow you to bring your child to class anymore. It's disruptive to the other students."

"Huh?"

She switches sides nervously, "It's out of my hands. The dean has sent a memo to all the teachers. You're going to have to find childcare if you want to continue."

I'm almost out of air, "ok."

I drag myself into the quad, blurry eyed with Khali on my back. I'm in a daze walking in the heat, tired, and frustrated, foot halfway in school, halfway out, broke and worn down. I'm assed out. I swim against the tide of happy go lucky, smiling, giggling, backpack wearing students who act like life is a breeze. I watch my Bridge program peers gathering outside the classrooms waiting for class to start. I walk past the Admissions building where I first got the seeds for education planted in the ground. Passion is now growing inside me, and hope is beating in my heart. But I'm at a loss for words. Now that I have the taste in my mouth, I'm hungry for knowledge. I want the books, the classes, the 12-block walk to campus, long winded teachers, expensive ass books. I feel sick to my stomach that it's over for me. I don't know why I thought I could be a student anyway.

I leave campus and wander downtown and get swallowed by the traffic of people once again invisible. I look at the homeless people eating out of trash cans and see the dejected spirits exiting the impatient AC transit buses and I have a familiar thought, *I hate Oakland.* Oakland is eating me alive. It inhales ambition and dreams and exhales hopelessness. I'm standing in the bowels of poverty on top of pigeon shit covered sidewalks when I see a young boy about five or six struggling to lift himself and his crutches onto the city bus. Nobody helps him. It ain't no love here.

I fall into the Aid office. I don't know why but I figured they could help me. I wait in line almost an hour before I can ask one simple question, "Do ya'll got anything to help with childcare?" She points me to a window, "There's a program called Bananas that gives vouchers out. But the waiting list is long."

I sit in the Bananas office for another 45 minutes with Khali pulling on my African shell necklace. I sit picking at my peeling fingernail polish while time passes slow as a check on the 1st and 15th. They call my name. The worker smiles at me. I hand her my application. By now I'm a pro at making my application

146

look like the sorriest piece of shit life. I don't have money. I don't have help. She adds me to her case load but tells me, "I have to be honest with you, the list is almost a year long." I sink even further, "A year?" The reality of it all lodges in my throat and it's hard to swallow. She smirks like she feels my pain. I want her to hold my suffering in her hand, to walk in my aching shoes for the last year of my life and see where I've come from. I want to spit fire and burn her ass up on her desk. I have carried my grades with me since the day I first got them thinking I was somebody. I've been so proud of myself. I toss my grades on her desk and let her take it in for a second. She sighs and looks up at this 20-year-old mother in front of her. I can see that she really does feel what I'm saying when I tell her, "I never made grades like this. I don't want to leave school."

I walk out with a year of childcare paid for by the State of California. My spirit rises like sunshine.

28: The rainbow is enuf

Thanksgiving is a feast of good friends and good food. There's bowls of jokes and pans of memories. We all lay around, after the sweet potatoes and coleslaw, after the cornbread dressing and Mac N Cheese, after the burping and dozing and drinking and laughing. Tia's standing up with a big white shirt over her pregnant belly and a glass of Cool-aid. Yusef is munching on corn and serving up his ghetto philosophes on life, "See sister's you got to get off the system. The welfare system is designed to destroy the black family structure." Delana laughs, "You sure like the systems turkey and dressing my BRUTHA."

I've overdosed on sweets and delicious words. Peaches has a sugary Keith Sweat song on her lips throwing down her hand in cards while her Acorn homies pass a ½ empty bottle of Vodka around with sauce hearty laughter. I serve the war vet from school a man-sized plate of dessert and plop down balancing a slice of pie on a Styrofoam plate on my knees. Maceo swings by with his 3 sons and adds them to the tribe of kids we have in here already.

He yells at me from the doorway, "I know my patna cooked!" *Damn right.* I made my mom's special lemon meringue pie and he doesn't even need an invite to dig in. Khali rips his clothes off and jumps in the Tonka car next to Tia's daughter butt naked. We all fall out laughing. I look around me and fall in love with Oakland again. I love this crazy ass family I've pieced together. This moment is like the rainbow after the rain. This is how we do it.

But the butterflies in my stomach are going crazy. I finally fit in somewhere. I'm home. But I have an announcement tearing at me. I got a Dear John letter I need to open up and read to my friends. This is Algebra hard. I take a breath and interrupt the different conversations going on, "Aye I got something to tell y'all."

Yusef laughs, "What? You pregnant?"

"Hell naw." I give him the side-eye. Then I get back to the business at hand, "I just wanted to tell ya'll... I'm leaving." This is the end of the road.

Peaches stops playing her hand, "You moving out?"

Everyone is quiet now. I try to keep a smile but get to the nitty gritty, "I'm moving out of California." If this is food for thought, the aftertaste ain't what you want.

Everyone's confused. I clear my throat and hit them with the info, "I'm moving to Arkansas."

You could hear a pin drop. They got this *whatdafuckisthisabout* look. Tia finally breaks the silence with laughter, and everyone joins in. They start making jokes, "Sit yo black ass down!"

"You ain't going nowhere."

"Put that on something."

I put it on everything. I'm serious, "Naw ya'll for real. I'm getting up out of here." They think it's a wolf ticket. Peaches is the only one who knows I'm for real. She knows about my family in Arkansas. She looks hurt but smiles and says, "Do what you got to do. If I had family, I'd be on the 1st thing smoking too." Her words hang in the air like musical notes.

Tia is shaking her head. I think about her boyfriend serving his own mama crack and how me and Tia used the money to buy non-perishable items for her and the baby because they didn't have a fridge. She doesn't have family either. I'm like her for-real big sister.

Maceo's face drops. He's looking at me hard like he can't blink, "Are you serious?"

I nod, "Yep."

"Damn. What the fuck? Why?" He cuts me down like a machete, "You real scandalous for this."

I explain about my family and tell him, "I just can't do it here. I just feel like I can do better in Arkansas. I can go to school and really really do something."

Maceo's voice sounds weird, "Fuck it go."

I'm tired of dry hustling and scraping the bottom all the time. I'm tired of living on borrowed hope and stolen dreams.

Yusef shakes his head, "It's gonna cost you a grip to move out there. That's way across the country."

The rest of my friends are all trying to figure out where the hell is Arkansas, *Ain't it like the country? I bet it ain't nothing but white folks out there.* Tia looks disgusted, "You gone be all country and talkin funny."

I tell Yusef, "I got a school check." My Pell Grant came in. I got a $1200 check from the school. I'm going to use it all to move. I've thought about this. I've weighed it in my head. I know I am going to do it. I think back to the 5-year-old boy struggling to climb the stairs on the bus, "I just want my son to have something better. I think it will be good for us" *Knock on wood.*

They wave me off and go back to enjoying their food and conversations. I don't think they really believe me. They think I'm tripping. Maceo sits on the arm of the couch near me, "You serious?"

I look up, "Yep."

He looks so sad and I believe him when he says, "Damn I'm gon miss you. I'm gon miss yo ass for real. But I feel you. I'd leave too. I hate this shit. I hate Oakland" I can see it in his eyes. It's that hopelessness that chews on your soul and eats away at you little by little. I remember sitting on the stairs with him and Delana one night and out of the blue we all just decided to cry. We literally *decided* to cry. We made a pact that we were going to let ourselves cry for everybody we lost. I remember how when the tears started to flow, it was like a dam broke and we couldn't stop. We lost it. I can still picture Maceo sprawled on the floor sobbing uncontrollably with gut wrenching sounds from his core, red faced with veins pulsating from his forehead. Delana had her arms wrapped around her legs on the steps weeping and I was holding the post choking with tears. We cried like babies until all we had left was sniffles and finally dry heaves. I think about how in the end he rolled over wet faced and just lay there exhausted from unbottling so much despair. We been crying and burning on the inside with eternal fire for so long that we'd forgotten the origin of our tears. So, when he says he knows why I want to leave, I believe him. It's just we've been each other's company in misery for so many years, through thick and thin. They all think this whole moving thing is a figment of my imagination. The truth is I spent weeks tossing and turning in my sleep, shadow boxing my fears before I even decided to tell them. I'm tired of momentary happiness. I'm tired of stumbling through life. I'm tired of last dollar days.

Word has been on the street that I'm leaving. I got my ticket. Now old friends are stopping bye to wish me well or tell me I'm a damn fool. Delana lets me have it, "Girl what is wrong with you?" She has her son with her and she's firing up some weed while she shakes her head. She looks at me sideways when I walk Khali out because I don't want him to see her smoking. I'm changing. I know it and she knows it and it don't sit to well with either of us. She thinks I'm throwing in the towel too soon. I think I'm jumping off a cliff making my wings on the way down.
I've been packing all week. My plan is to leave by Christmas. I don't have much, I packed up my pain and hurt and mistrust. I got a shitload of regrets tucked into suitcases. I'm also taking all of Khali's things, one of the raggedy couches and some random dishes. Peaches and her friends will keep all the things undone, unpaid for, broken toys and torn up blinds. The other girls are sniping me with their gazes from across the room. Suinjata comes by to wish me well. He is still doing parties but has started selling sneakers and jerseys to make extra money. He hands me some cash, "If you need something just holla at me." I look at him with his girlfriend and think that if I ever fall in love again, I want it to be with a guy like him. I hug him and I feel him kiss my cheek. I realize it. I chose wrong.

When the moving company brings a truck and parks it in

the yard my friends go insane. Now they know it's real. Maceo tries to talk me out of it, breaking it down like an 8ball, raw and uncut "You don't know your family out there. Man, they ain't gone have no love for you like we do. If worse come to worse, you know who to call." He wanted me to know he was still stackin his paper.

He looks through my screen at the war vet, 'What about old boy?" The vet is my old man now. I took to him because he started taking my dirty clothes to his house and washing them for me, so I'd have clean clothes to wear to school. He bought my son a 49rs coat. He was convenient but he was a drug addict who was battling a court case. I look at him slouched on the sofa, "We cool. He don't want me to go but I'm going anyway."

Delana is beside herself, "On the real, you gonna get out there and want to come back. Maceo tell this fool."

I shake my head, "I doubt it." But deep down I was shaking with fear.

She's concerned, "So what you gone do if you get out there and can't make it?"

I shrug, "Do what I always do." Put one foot in front of the other and keep it moving. If I fail, I hope I can find my way back to Patti Labelle songs, chipped paint and a good game of dominos and spades.

But I'm going come hell or highwater. Delana laughs, "You gave up. I'm west side till I die." Tia co-signs, "and I betcha!"

Me too but something was calling to me from the south. I know it's country. I know it's slow-paced. But It's where my mother was born and raised. It's where my father bought his first house on Allis street when he was 21. It's where the wind is filled with my ancestors' cries. It's where I'm going to find myself.

Peaches is silent on the couch. She's already sung off her skirt and button-down shirt to Anita Baker's tape. The $5.00 an hour job she interviewed for has hired her and she catches the BART train every day to her new job, Bay Alarms. Now she's silently watching me pack while my friends stand around and complain. She has already told me that if she had family she would go too. She is the only one who has not said a negative thing. I can see that she wishes that she could pack up and leave too. I'm anxious but excited at the same time.

I pack some dishes, some pictures, a mattress, one couch and shit like that. I can't bag the love, the loyalty, home, family, God it's all just scattered around in smiles, embraces and kind words.

I get on the train at Amtrak's newly built Emeryville station. I have this weird feeling. I had a dream last night about traveling back in time. I dreamed that when I got off the station in little Rock it was the early 1900s and everything was black and white. I thought that I would panic but I step on the train and sit Khali in an empty seat. My mother sits in the seat facing us. She has a blanket and a pillow. I look out the window at Oakland, the hills, the Pacific Ocean and I feel homesick already. If home is where the heart is then mine is beating along the coastal sky where seagulls dip into the marina. For me the sun sets in the west, always. There's a chorus of voices in my head, 'You're stupid." "You're not going to like it." I have jarring flashbacks of my circle of friends. My memories comfort me, love me, sing me into restless sleep on the hard cushion seat of the train. Tia with her double barrel shotgun. Maceo rollin a blunt. Sweet Juice Peaches dancing, dancing away those Oakland blues.

I doze off with Khali snuggled up under a blanket beside me. When I wake up, we are passing through snowcapped mountains. I look out my window at the scenery. It doesn't snow in California.

I look at my mom sitting across from me, knees drawn up underneath an army blanket, hands like twisted roots. Her skin is corn whiskey brown. The wrinkles on her face seem deeper and more set in now. If a woman isn't loved does, she wither away? Does she rot away like a tree with no sun? I think about her traveling on a bus from Arkansas 1,955 miles to get me from Oakland. I watch her looking out of the window and for the first time she seems regal. I know now her love is measured in neckbones simmering on the stove and fresh lemon pies with

Jackson vanilla wafer crushed into butter. I always seemed to dance to music she couldn't hear. No matter how much I jumped and thrashed and waved my arms. She gives me a timid smile. She's not a city girl. I know in the South she can tell time with lighting bugs and the moonshine song of crickets. I wonder what childhood memories she has tightened up in her mind like a mason jar. I'm happy that she went home. I want to see her within the context of her own life. I want to know what her childhood was like. I know her memory runs deep as the Arkansas river and I want to stand on its banks and wet my feet in the waters. I never knew my mother's mother who was buried in the word when my mother was only 3 years old. I've spent 21 years trying to find her in the wilderness of my mother. A lot of the time we see the scars but not the pain. As Rumi says, the wound is the place where the Light enters you." I get it. I start to understand that her womanhood is rooted in endurance and quiet resolve. I've watched my mother walking barefoot on broken pieces and act like it doesn't hurt. That she opens her eyes each day to a new sunrise and goes on to hammer away at the stone and dig herself out with her bare hands, is bravery. Every woman has to fight herself free. That she dances in summer thunderstorms and hums spiritual songs unconsciously. Her life is her story and I am the encore. I look at her and see my reflection. I celebrate her with every new chapter of my life.   I think about seeing my father again, his southern drawl like an acoustic guitar; hot and humid like the air. I want to sit under him like a big oak tree and feel protected from the world. I want my son to play in the yard that's fertilized by his grandfather's sweat and tears. I sit on the train with my stomach in knots, on the brink of new possibilities. I think about my Uncle and how he picked bits and pieces of me when I was too young to fight him off. I want my things back. I know I'm going to visit him, in his home with his wife. I'm going to reach into his heart and snatch back my innocence and restore myself into who I was. I'm going to complete the circle. I've already told my mother my plans. Her eyes grew heavy with sadness, but I thought I see a glimmer of admiration. I curl up in the pages of a book of Gwendolyn Brook's poems. She speaks to me, "even if you're not ready for day, it cannot always be night."

We make it to Little Rock in 3 days. I call Delana to tell her that I have finally made it. Aside from the stifling heat and biting mosquitos I think I am going to be just fine.
"Hey Girl. I'm out here with these big ass cockroaches."
She doesn't laugh. Her voice is muddy, calmed with herb, "They killed Maceo. He got shot in Berkeley. He's gone" It hits me like a thunderbolt.
A wave runs through my body. I can't respond.
"Hello? Hello?"
I'm flooded with emotions and images of a young Maceo with eyes like wildfire. *They* erased years and months and days in a matter of minutes? My African-Indian Berkeley Man? I can't even imagine it. He had the blood of Berkeley running through his veins, *He loved Berkeley.* Khali is pulling on my leg raising his sippy cup. I sit on the bed and cradle my phone and almost whisper "What happened? "Her words fire shots of images of gunfire and him choking on his own blood. His laughter ricochets in my room. The vision of his smiling face, now memorialized as a memory, goes on forever like the horizon over the Pacific Ocean.
She tells me he was shot in broad daylight on Durant Road near UC Berkeley while college students gathered for lunch. He and his baby mother went to grab a bite and a guy opened fire on them, hitting him in the throat and another guy in the chest. His girlfriend tried unsuccessfully to pull him into her car. Delana says she watched her screaming and crying on the news with his blood all over her. His body lay on the concrete, under a sheet for three hours while the cops waited on the coroner. The newscaster stated simply, "A gangbanger, ex-felon was gunned down outside of Top Dog eatery today. But in other news...." I'm disgusted at the coverage. Sadness rains down on me. I remember him laying his head on my chest in the midst of all that chaos. I remember that moment of peace and stillness. I hang up the phone and cry until I'm sick trying to will back yesterday. I let grief wash over me

like water pounding into the rocks at the marina. I want my friend back. I already miss the music of his voice sounding sweet as penny candy in my ear, "I'm so glad we have this." The news made it quite clear that we were the only ones who thought he was alive. He had been dead to them a long time ago, swallowed up, buried alive by a city he loved. Even after I packed and moved, I knew the truth would come after me.

Epilogue.

Most stories start with the beginning and end with the end. My story starts from the end and works it was to a new beginning. Little by little I began to realize that I escaped a hell that has so many of us trapped inside its walls. I was in a prison of low mentality and low self-worth. It wasn't Oakland that held me captive. It wasn't Arkansas that set me free. It was opening my mind to the possibilities that lay ahead of me. I came to understand that success is measured, not from where you are but, from where you came from. The love we share is an unsophisticated loan-me $5 kinda love. I often feel the pain and worthlessness I felt growing up biting and nipping at my back. I spoke with Suinjata regarding Maceo's death and he said something that stung me deeply, "Jen we been dying. I'm just glad you left." It was the first time that anyone ever acknowledged that I saved my own life. We were all drowning in the unfair circumstances of our lives. I had lunged into the water and beat against the waves until I found solid ground. No one could have done it for me. Maceo's death was a hurt that shot down into my soul, that ripped my gut right out of me. It wasn't just his physical death but the realization that his death signaled the beginning of my departure from my past life. I was leaving myself behind. I was burying all those things that I thought made me who I was. My first job in Arkansas was a key holder at Camelot records where I took night deposits to Bank of America. During which time Peaches commented, "They don't know who they are fucking with," and they really didn't. But my reality had shifted. I was such a long way gone from who I used to be. In the end you only wind up stealing from yourself. I wasn't a thief. I wasn't a welfare recipient. I wasn't a hood rat. I was a Black Girl who was Lost but who had challenged the reflection I saw in the mirror. I learned that a rose called by any other name may struggle to blossom, but it is still truly a rose. This book is my celebration of these flowers, those broken, damaged bushels pushing through the cracks in the concrete. Most of the young women I bonded with were motherless children from broken homes who struggled to piece together what it means to be a mother from scraps and fragments of female role models that sometimes came in the form of a peer. I knew girls who built a house out of bits and pieces. Most of us have deeply rooted secrets of molestation and abuse that shakes the family tree apart. Many of us used whatever tools we could rig up to survive on the front lines of an urban war zone that nobody even acknowledges and still deal with post-traumatic stress as do a lot of young women on this journey to womanhood. Still, the war inside us was harder to conquer. The essence of womanhood is in every day, every small struggle, every forced smile. And even though I find myself still laughing and grabbing at old memories that are still alive in my mind, I know that I am different now. I also know I've seen roses in full bloom where flowers aren't even supposed to grow.

But I love you Oakland
My sunny California
Where I had my first real kiss
Breathed my first sigh of heartache
I love your rugged shore
Your purple sunsets
Half your beauties are untold
But I keep your memories on repeat.

Maceo had three sons, the oldest carries his features and his name. I look at pictures of Maceo Jr and my stomach tightens with memories of his pop in his snap-back raiders cap and white denim standing out on the field at Emery high his eyes dazzling with life. Sometimes I catch a glimpse of him in somebody's eyes or see him in a stranger's smile. Some things you just can't leave behind.

Suinjata had a son and opened his own store in Oakland where he sells clothes and shoes. He still DJ's and we still stay in touch.

Tia went to jail for cashing fake payroll checks and ultimately lost custody of her children. She eventually fought her way back to society and took on a job at the Cheesecake Factory where she would work for 11 yrs. before moving on. I always thought that losing her mother at such an early age played a major role in her finding her footing. Her own daughter became a teenage mom at 16.

Delana still lives in West Oakland and spends her time writing and supporting her son who was charged as an adult with murder and sent to prison for 25+ years.

Amini finished school and began working in a salon where she makes money to raise her daughter as a single parent and spends her days watching her beloved twist and turn as a dancer in an Oakland based dance company.

I lost contact with Yusef, but I imagine he is somewhere raising a family and probably reciting the Qur'an to his children somewhere on the outskirts of Oakland.

Almost twenty years later, I still talk to Peaches almost every day in our Oaklandish way with our words quick and bumping into each other. That scrawny daughter of hers has grown into a beautiful woman. Peaches raised her and a son as a single mother. That $5 an hour job catapulted her into the workplace. That drive and determination that had her waking at dawn and catching the bus all over Oakland was what has kept her competitively in the workforce and finally was promoted to leadership position. I will always remember her rising from the couch and stepping out into the world each day demanding someone to see her. She now works for a major California company making a six-figure salary. She has never stopped working.

I began the process of sorting out my relationship with my mother. Thru many conversations we struggle to put together the pieces of the broken homes, dysfunctional relationships and lack of self-worth that has plagued women in my family probably centuries before I was even born. My mother dealt with mental health issues and depression and eventually sought professional help. I imagine that losing her own mother at such a young age played a huge part in why the mother/daughter connection between us was fractured. It was akin to building a bridge over troubled waters.

As for me, I continued my pursuit of higher education and received an English Degree with Writing as my minor. I began to write myself into existence with my stories of perseverance. In retrospect I understand my journey. Khali, my first born was my sun, without him there was no light. I gave birth to my second son, Daniel. I taught myself to drive and got my license. I drive a Honda Accord and own a small 3-bedroom home in South West Little Rock with a small fenced in backyard and one car garage with my husband. I wake up Sunday mornings, draw back my curtains and let the sun in. I play oldies that me and Peaches used to boogie down to and for a moment I'm back on E14th street wrapped in musical notes. I look at my son Khali, a grown man, standing 6 feet tall and I think to myself, "We did it."
You have to measure your success from where you came from.

COFFY DAVIS

Coffy Davis is the Director and founder of The Underground Railroad Neighborhood Project (T.U.R.N. project) and the director of the original lyrical stage play *FREEDOM*. A nationally known poet, playwright, author and producer, she is the 2017 Arkansas Arts Council Fellowship Award winner for Creative Non-Fiction for the book *MEdusa*. Davis is the Author of the book FREEDOM and the Cd's *Ghetto Politics, Eclipse* and *Freedom*. In 2013 her film *Loyalty* opened at the Rivendale theater in Little Rock, Arkansas. She has performed Spoken word poetry in various venues across the US and competed and placed in National slams with the poetry troupe *Foreign Tongues*.

She is the proud mother of Khali and youngest son Daniel who was born of the 20-year union of her and husband Danny. She resides in Little Rock, AR.

Made in the USA
Columbia, SC
05 November 2021

48402448R00107